Cryptosup

Being a supplement to A Dictionary of Cryptozoology

by

Ronan Coghlan

BANGOR:
Xiphos Books
2005.

First Edition.

Published by
Xiphos Books,
1, Hillside Gardens,
BANGOR,
BT19 6SJ.
Northern Ireland.

ISBN: 0-9544936-4-8

Introduction:
What is *Cryptosup?*

Way back in the good old days – 2004, to be precise – the present writer produced a *Dictionary of Cryptozoology*, largely because a cheap but comprehensive volume on this subject was a desideratum. However, such a volume needs constant updating. New discoveries occur, new cryptids are reported. Even creatures thought extinct are found not to be so, as in the case of the ivory-billed woodpecker. That is why *Cryptosup* has been produced. I look forward to any input from readers, except for Scornful Missives, for I am of a Sensitive Disposition.

Insofar as Alien Big Cats are mentioned in this work, there are so many referred to at present that I have generally refrained from listing creatures that appear to be black panthers or pumas, but have confined myself mainly to those showing characteristics featured by neither of these species.

Ronan Coghlan

As this forms a supplement to *A Dictionary of Cryptozoology*, the same numbers and letters for source references are used. New source references will be found at the back. References simply to *Dictionary* refer to the main dictionary. I have not hesitated to mention a number of cryptobotanic items in the listing, even if these are a little beyond the true boundaries of a work on cryptozoology. I have not featured some supernatural beings such as the African tokoloshe .

Abbreviations

ABC = alien big cat, i.e., a large mystery feline animal
BHM = big hairy monster, such as the yeti, Bigfoot, etc.
CFZ=Centre for Fortean Zoology (Exeter, England)

ABAIA Huge eel found in lakes according to Melanesian legend. [120]

ABASS Term used for a BHM in northern Siberia. [183]

ACHIYALATOPA Gigantic monster with flint feathers in Zuñi myth.

ADAHAN WILDMAN This creature was captured in Turkey in 1938. It was vegetarian and unable to talk. It showed a fear of man. Just what it was remains a mystery.[155]

ADANDARA In Azande myth, a kind of wild cat that hunts at night. It is regarded as a witchcraft animal. The males have relations with women who sometimes give birth to kittens. [K5]

ADARNA Magical bird of Filipino legend. Like the phoenix, there seems to be only a single specimen. [K7]

AFRICAN ONE-HORNED RHINOCEROS African rhinoceroses are supposed to have two horns, but sightings of single-horned specimens were reported in days gone by. These could, of course, have been freaks.

AGTA Hairy hominid in Filipino lore, 8-9' tall. [183]

ALBANIAN According to Pliny, albanians were crypto-humans. In most ways they seem to have looked like humans, but they had the eyes of owls. Do not confuse with Albanians of Albania.

ALBAWITCH A humanoid found in the woods near Columbia (Pa.). North of that town is Chickies Rock, one of their haunts. The creatures seem to be largely arboreal. They are supposed to have become extinct or nearly so in the 19th Century. They have (or had) a taste for apples. [177]

ALCESTER ADDER A legendary giant viper that killed a man in this Warwickshire town in 1544. [C1]

ALESUND SEA SERPENT A. Molvaer filmed a sea serpent eating a dead whale in a fjord at this Norwegian locale in 1999. It was 25-30m long. The head was large, the neck long. Zoological experts consulted did not think highly of the film. [34]

ALOES In Thevet's *Cosmographie universelle* (1575), this curious fish is reported from the New World. When it swims on the water, it resembles a goose, its long neck sticking into the air.

ALPINE LIZARD Unidentified large lizards with short legs have been reported in the Italian Alps. It hardly seems possible we are dealing with tatzelworms here. [155]

AMERICAN GIANT There are various traditions amongst the Native Americans of races of giants inhabiting their continent. These include the Ronnongwetowanea of the Iroquois, the Tsunil'kalu of the Cherokee, the Wong-a-Rouskah-Podarouhuh-Poruh-Wah-Roughea-Ga of the Winnebago, the Tshawbitts of the Shoshone and the Natliskeliguten of the Salish. There have also been various reports of the graves of giant humans being discovered on American soil.

AMES GIANT SNAKE A 25' long snake shot on a farm at Ames (Texas) in 1982. However, when the farmer went to collect the carcass, it was not to be found. The beast, perchance, had not been killed.

ANTARCTIC HUMANOID Such a creature, shambling of gait and covered in hair, has, on one occasion, been reported near a research station on the world's most inhospitable continent. It has been claimed that large white humanoid bodies have been seen in Antarctic waters. [D10 85]

ANZU In Mesopotamian myth, a huge bird with the head of a lion.

APODA A Mexican footless bird which had to use strings or feathers to balance itself on trees, according to J. de Acosta in 1581. The bird's name was coined by Linnaeus. [H17]

AQUATIC BAT A flightless water-dwelling bat reported from the Amazon Basin. [180]

ARKANSAS SNAKE A 30' long snake of mysterious origin reported from Little River County (Arkansas). [12]

ARKANSAS WILDMAN The *Memphis Enquirer* reports a sighting in March, 1851, of this creature, which it claimed was well known in St Francis Green and Poinsett counties.

ARMOURED FISH A large armoured and unidentified piscid reported from Lake Como, Italy. [155]

ARMOUR-PLATED FISH A strange fish with a sucker for a mouth washed up at St Petersburg (Florida). [165]

ASEKA-MOKE A river-dwelling monster, supposedly found in Africa. [179]

AUCKLAND CREATURE *see* **Domain Creature.**

AUGHNACLOY FLYING CREATURE A dinosaur-like bird (?pterosaur) seen by a child at Aughnacloy, Ireland, one Hallowe'en. It made a squawking noise. It may be remembered that at the Irish and Scottish festival of Hallowe'en (*Oíche Shamna*), it is believed the portal to the Otherworld is open. [#1]

AUSTRALIAN CAMEL Camels were introduced into Australia in 1840. There are some Aboriginal reports of them prior to this. This could mean there is a native species, but, in the light of Australian fauna generally, this seems very unlikely. It may be there were some unrecorded importations.

AUSTRALIAN WATER SNAKE A huge snake that looks like a python, which lives in the water, according to Aboriginal lore. [#9]

AUSTRIAN FLYING SNAKE These were to be found in Styria in the 16th Century, Gesner informs us.

AVDOSHKA Russian term used in the vicinity of Novgorod for a BHM. [183]

AYR CAT Large mystery cat seen in a garden in Ayr, Scotland, in 1969. It had stripes like a tiger, but wasn't one. Instead, it looked like a giant domestic cat. [167]

BAGAT A preternatural dog, harmless generally if left alone, in Filipino folklore.

BAJADA GRANDE BEAST A three-eyed white-haired monster that reportedly attacked an Argentine motor-cyclist in 1968. [A4]

BALAUR A creature like, but distinct from, a dragon in Romanian legends. It is thought to have a number of heads. [152]

BALI(N) A huge monkey of Indian legend, killed by Rama. [K6]

BALTIC SEA SERPENTS A number of sea serpents have been spotted in the Baltic Sea. A pair were seen together near Stockholm in 1920. [32]

BANFF SEA SERPENT This noisy creature was reported by seamen in 1896. It was 300' long and had three humps. It was seen off the Scottish coast. [146]

BARMI-BIRGOO Apelike creature of Australian lore.

BARREGO VALLEY SANDMAN According to the *Hollow Earth Insider* website, in this area of California in 1964 V. Stoyanow noticed several BHM-type footprints leading underground, as though some form of subterranean bigfoot were to be found in the area.

BAT BOY According to tabloid articles in the United States, this creature was captured in West Virginia. It was 2' tall, very vicious, could see in the dark and had ears like radar equipment. It was kept in a centre at Wheeling, but escaped and flew to Las Vegas, where it was recaptured. The story has inspired a musical.

BAY CITY FLYING REPTILE This creature apparently flew from a tree to a fence 35' away at this Texas location. There were supposedly two witnesses.

BEAR BOOGER East Kentucky name for a BHM.

BEAR-HEADED MAN A creature, able to talk, allegedly seen in the west of Ireland, but details of date and witness are lacking. It is supposed to have told the witness not to talk to it. [146]

BEAST OF AUXERROIS A mystery predator on the loose in this part of France in 1731-4. Another was at large in the same region in 1817. [155]

BEAST OF BALA A large beast reported from North Wales in 1997. It was white and catlike. [163]

BEAST OF BOSNIA Strange animal whose dead body has been photographed. Although it is unidentifiable, it may be a skinned marten. [2]

BEAST OF BYNOE Creature resembling a plesiosaur said to be found in Bynoe Bay, near Darwin (Northern Territory), Australia. [120]

BEAST OF CWMBRAN A creature resembling a black panther photographed in this part of Wales in 2005. ABC reports have been coming in from this area for about two years.

BEAST OF GREEN DRIVE If descriptions are to be believed, an extraordinary beast lurks in Lytham St Annes (Lancs). A drawing based on descriptions by S. Shearon in the *Lytham St Annes Express* shows a creature with a lean body, long ears and claws. It is supposed to be about the size of a Labrador. It was first reported in 2005. [175]

BEAST OF RYEDALE Badger-sized black beast observed in Britain in 2003. [184]

BEAST OF SIZERGH CASTLE Large chocolate-black creature which looked a little deerlike but was hoofless. It was seen in this location in Lancashire. [85]

BEAST OF VIVARAIS A mystery beast in France on the rampage from 1809-1816. [155]

BEASTIE OF BUTTS COURT A mystery animal which appears to be some kind of rodent, spotted on the prowl in Leeds (Yorkshire) in April, 2005. Its front legs are like a squirrel's, it has whiskers and is said to be too large to be a rat. It has been suggested it is a degu (*Octodon degus*).

BENN EDAIR SERPENT A monster of Irish mythology, killed by the hero Finn. Benn Edair is modern Howth (Co Dublin).

BERGEN COUNTY CREATURE A strange creature seen in Bergen County (New Jersey) by a child in 1959. Opening a door, he happened on a brown creature, fat, furry and about 3.5' tall with hypnotic red eyes. [154]

BERKELEY LAKE TURTLE A huge turtle reported from this lake in Georgia. It exceeds the size of any known turtle in the state fauna.

BERKELEY TOAD A huge toad which, according to legend, was discovered in an oubliette in Berkeley Castle, Gloucestershire, in the reign of Henry VII (1485-1509). [H15]

BI BI Winged fox allegedly found in China. [A4]

BIG BLACK THING This vague term is used to signify an unidentified animal seen in Illinois. Some children claimed it was the size of a cow with doglike ears. On one occasion a group of four of the creatures was observed. As all of this is so vague, more than one kind of creature may be involved. [161]

BIG CENTIPEDE Monstrous being of Navaho legend, born from the blood of earlier monsters. [R8]

BIG ED Oklahoma name for a BHM.

BIG MAN Term used by some Amerindians for a BHM.

BIG SWAN POND MONSTER In 1892 a monster looking like a serpent with the head of a dog was reported by a number of witnesses in this Indiana lake. Its skin was red and white [#19]

BIGFOOT *Add to Dictionary article:* The Patterson-Gimlin film's authenticity has been challenged in a recent book, *The Making of Bigfoot* (2004) by G. Long. The findings of this volume have in turn been challenged by other Bigfoot experts. Kinesiologist Jurgen Konczak (Minnesota University) has opined that the walk of the creature in the film is neither a human nor a pithecoid gait and, if it is only a human in an ape suit, he has managed to progress in a singularly skilful manner. A videotape allegedly of bigfoot was taken at Norway House (Manitoba) in April, 2005. The image on the tape does not seem very clear. As we write, there is word of an expedition to capture a bigfoot. Led by C. Thomas Biscardi, it will search in the Happy Camp area of California. Hair, allegedly from a bigfoot, is to be analysed by the University of Alberta.

BILINGTON HUMANOID This was reported by two schoolgirls near Bilington (Kent) in 1969. [146]

BIPEDAL CREATURE Such a creature, looking like a tiger (?jaguar), was disturbed killing hens by their owner at Leona Vicario (Yucatan), Mexico. [1]

BIRDMAN Strange creature active in Ashland (Kentucky) in 1967. It was blamed for the killing of livestock and for screams heard in the night. It is also supposed to have entered a house and to have been seen making its way up some stairs. [174]

BISCIONE The big snake which is an heraldic device of the city of Milan. It was supposedly a dragon called Tarantasio, killed by a member of the Visconti family. [2]

BLACK BOBCAT An animal that resembled a bobcat, black except for a white paw, seen by the compiler of the *Encyclopedia Lurkanica* in Florida. [179]

BLACK ORANG-UTAN Early reports of the orang-utan suggest that some of them belong or belonged to a black colour variation. [A5]

BLOB *Add to Dictionary article:* It now seems clear that at least some blobs are the remains of decomposing whales.

BLOOD SUCKER Name given by schoolchildren in Hong Kong to some kind of arthropod, about 1.5" in length. While its identity remains uncertain, it may be the young of some kind of mantis. [1]

BLUE BABY Although my information here is vague and uncertain, I am putting it in before going to press because of its singularity. Apparently fishermen off the Irish coast picked up a fish or mammal that looked like a blue baby. It was like nothing they had seen before, so they released it back into the water. I have no information regarding the date or location of this incident. My informant, Gary Cunningham, is going to try to elicit further information, as he knows one of the men concerned.

BOA NEGRO, EL Gigantic black snake reported from the Amazon region. [2]

BODACH A kind of small seal in the lore of the Highlands of Scotland in the early 19th Century. If it ever existed, it may be extinct today. [A5]

BOJI Hairy giants of Colorado. They were generally thought to be primates, though one witness held they were an unknown species of bear. [183]

BOMERE POOL FISH A monster fish in Shropshire folklore, armed with a sword which it uses to cut through fishermen's nets.

BOO-BAGGER In white American lore, a hairy creature that seems to combine traits of human and bear. It is supposedly found in the northwestern USA and also western Canada. [G10]

BRACKEN COUNTY CREATURES A creature whose head was variously described as being like that of an elephant, horse, etc., gigantic and shaggy, with large paws, claws, cloven hooves, horns and a dart-shaped end to its tail was supposedly on the rampage in Bracken County (Kentucky) in 1866. A 6' tall creature, with hair and tail composed of flame, resembling a man above the waist and a horse below, exuding fiery breath, was reported in the same county in 1868. [#7]

BRAZILIAN FLYING HUMANOIDS These were observed at Pelotas, Brazil, in the 1950s. They were described as resembling men and they were about 6' tall.

BRAZILIAN HUMANOID In 2004 one Alan Flavio disturbed a humanoid at night. It had thin legs and a colour reminiscent of graphite. It fled, but later entered his bedroom, paralysing him by placing a hand on his chest. This occurred near Joao Pessoa (Brazil).

BREYDEABACH'S APE A kind of ape mentioned by Gesner. The accompanying illustration in his book shows it plying a walking-stick. [179]

BRITISH BEAVER Although the beaver has been extinct in Britain for many a century, there are now some said to be dwelling in the backwaters of the River Axe, where they have built dams. They may be breeding. [#1]

BRITISH GARTER SNAKE The garter snake is usually found in parts transatlantic, but reports of them surfaced in Dorset in the 1980s. [C1]

BRITISH THYLACINE A cryptid in its native Australia, one was apparently observed near Branksane (Dorset) in 1974. [146]

BROAD TOP SNAKE Gigantic serpent which many claim to have seen in Pennsylvania. Some suggest it lurks in coal mines. There have been sightings since 1919. A woman who saw one of the snakes in 1987 estimated that it exceeded 22'. It had the rotundity of a python. Three men in a truck reported seeing one in 2000. [2 R6 A5]

BUDA A werehyena in the lore of Ethiopia. The name is taken from the Buda tribe, skilled in smithcraft, which is said to number many werehyenas amongst its members, but the term is applied even to werehyenas not of this tribe. [H16]

BULL MAN Apparently a man with the power to turn himself into a bull, who was a bell ringer at Woolwich and was much beloved locally. [H16]

BULGARIAN FLYING CREATURE A number of these were seen in 1947 by a single youthful observer. They looked not unlike sticks or snakes, but, if they were snakes, they moved in a most unserpentine fashion, in a straight line. Then they flew off and were lost to sight behind some trees. [155]

BUNDJA BUNDJA GANGA Hairy wildman of Australian Aboriginal lore, said to live in Queensland. Some are of human height, some larger. They live in caves. [G11]

BURAKA Creatures in Hausa belief. A buraka has a man's head, a horse's legs and feet and can fly. [12]

BUSH APE Alternative name for the yowie.

CAC DI'TS'INI A monster known as the Bony Bear in Navaho myth. [R8]

CAC NA'ALKA'HI Known as the Tracking Bear, this monster of Navaho myth lived in a mountain cave. [R8]

CADDINGTON CREATURE This was seen near Luton, England, about 1981. A creature about 8' in height which seemed to combine features of man, bird and bear and which seemed to levitate on yellow light was observed. The witnesses fled into a tunnel, which was protected by an iron grille which had an opening large enough to accommodate them. They heard behind them what seemed to be the creature shaking the grille and screaming. The exact location of the encounter was Bluebell Wood. [#1]

CALEDONIA BIRD In 1948 a huge bird, bigger than an aeroplane, was reported at

Caledonia (Illinois). [161]

CALLITRICE A bearded humanoid with a tail, of which Pliny speaks. The curious observer, he informs us, may find them in Ethiopia.

CALOPUS This creature has horns like a ram's. It also has features compared with those of a wolf, boar, etc., and exists in the lore of Iran. [A4]

CAMELON CAT An orange cat the size of a lion with a partially white tail seen in Scotland in 2002. [167]

CAMOODI Found in the rivers of South America, this is said to be a giant horned reptile. [179]

CAMUENARE A giant monkey said to be found in South America. [179]

CARLISLE DINOSAUR On the tomb in Carlisle (Cumbria) of Bishop Bell (15th Century) is a carving of what looks startlingly like a sauropod dinosaur. The question that arises is whether it is based on a real original. [180]

CAX-VINIC *Add to Dictionary article:* It cannot be said with certainty that the cax-vinic and salvaje are identical.

CANTON BIRD In 2002 this bird, estimated wingspan 15-20', was espied by three men near Canton (Illinois). [161]

CAPPY *Add to Dictionary article:* There appears to be a story that this monster was captured and taken away by an African scientist.

CARDRONA CAT Two mystery ABCs, white in colour, were seen at this Scottish locale in 2003. There had been earlier sightings. [167]

CARSKA BARA CREATURE Large creature resembling a squid said to be found in the Carska Bara Swamp in Serbia. [#9]

CARSON LIZARD Near Carson (California) in 1975, a giant lizard with a humped back was seen by motorists crossing the San Diego Freeway. [R6]

CASCADE SNAKE A giant snake, 20'-30' long, which was hit by a motorist near Cascade (Indiana) in 1978. The snake was not there when she returned to the scene of the incident. There had been other reports of the animal. [R6]

CASPIAN FISH MAN A manlike beast with arms, a beak like a dolphin's, fins and hair has been reported by *Pravda* to have been seen in the Caspian Sea, the world's largest lake. He is called in Farsi *Runan-shah,* 'sea king'. [120 1]

CASPIAN TIGER *Add to Dictionary article:* With regard to this allegedly extinct subspecies, there is a rumour that one was shot in Afghanistan in 1997. [1]

CAPE BONAVISTA SEA MONSTER Strange creature – or perhaps an inanimate object – seen off Newfoundland in 2000. [165]

CAT MAN A black hairy creature with some human-like characteristics supposed to be found in Maryland in the environs of the Wicomico River. [R6]

CAT-BOBCAT HYBRID It is received wisdom amongst geneticists that these two animals cannot be crossed, but it has also been alleged they have been.

CATGAROOKEY Name given to a mystery animal reported in Salisbury (Wilts) by the *Sun*. It was described as having characteristics of cat, kangaroo and monkey. Witness R. Clark suggested it might have been a coati. If so, it would not be the only case of a coati's being found wild in Britain.

CATOCTIN DRAGON A dragon reported in the Catoctin Mountains by a resident of Frederick (Maryland) in 1883. It was of monstrous size and its eyeballs glared. [N]

CAYUGA LAKE MONSTER A beast known as "Old Greeny". A monster has been reported in this lake in New York state since 1897 and a couple of such beasts were observed in 1929. They were described as being 12-15' long.   [120]

CEASG A kind of mermaid, half human, half salmon, in Scottish folklore. The myth of the external soul, i.e., a soul kept in some place outside the body, is attached to this creature. [P3]

CENTICORE Alternative name for the yale.

CENTIPEDE This is not the small insect so called, but a huge monster of Japanese legend, slain by the hero Hidesato by shooting it with an arrow. [K7]

CERAM CIVET Possible new species of civet sighted in Ceram, Indonesia, in 1986.

CHAC Term used for a dragon in Yucatan.

CHAD BEAST This was described by F. Fresnel in 1843. The animal looked like a bull, its legs were like an elephant's, it sported a single horn (which it could move about) and it lived in Chad.

CHALK POINT MONSTER Maryland term for a BHM.

CHAMPLAIN'S BIRD Bird seen by Samuel de Champlain (1567-1635) in Ontario. It had a psittacine beak, a red head, blue wings and a yellow body. [H17]

CHAMROSH Firdausi, the great epic poet of Iran, tells us of this bird in his monumental *Shah-Namah* (Book of Kings). It dwelt on Mount Elburz and guarded the land of Persia from invaders.

CHARBURY CREATURE Bear-like creature which crossed the road at Charbury,

England, in 2000. It was seen by a bus driver and another witness. It was later reported standing at the roadside. [187]

CHARD BIRD A gigantic bird with a 14' wingspan reported over Chard (Somerset) in 1975. [146]

CHARLOTTE CREATURE A creature reported from near Charlotte (North Carolina) said to have a woman's face and a feline body. [R6]

CHARYBDIS Sea monster of Greek mythology, which in origin seems to have been merely a whirlpool.

CHAT-HUANT Canadian bird said to be a mixture of cat and owl, which would capture mice, fatten them up by feeding them and then eat them. [H17]

CHIAMAY FLYING SNAKE The writer Borchart (1599-1667) claims there are flying serpents in this area. He is not sure, however, where this area is, but thinks it is Chamonix (France).

CHICKLY CUDLY Human-creature with a terrapin-like head, big eyes and a big nose, noted in the United States in 1793.

CHIOGGIA SEA MONSTER A creature that looked like a whale but boasted a porcine snout was captured at this Italian location in 1889. [155]

CHOANITO Wenatchee Indian name for a BHM.

CHUPACABRAS *Add to Dictionary article:* Some confusion exists over the name of this creature. In standard Spanish it would be *chupacabras*, while *chupacabra* would be a substandard, if widely used, colloquialism. The word was invented by two friends, one of whom was Ismael Agauyo of the Canovenas Civil Defense in Puerto Rico.

CICERO MOTHMAN This was reported by a witness in Cicero (Illinois). It was described as huge and black. The witness had been in a trance out of which he alleged the mothman snapped him. [174]

CIROGRILLUS Creature mentioned by Aesop, perhaps an unknown kind of hedgehog or porcupine.

CLOUGHTON CREATURE An animal like a small bear with a hump and short legs sighted in Yorkshire in 1993. [184]

CLUTCHBONE A creature said to have a fiery head set in a material collar and leathery black skin. Its height is 190cm-230cm. It is dangerous and may dismember victims. The earliest accounts, from northern England, seem to date from around 1800. [152]

COJE YA MENA Mystery animal of Angola. It is said to be smaller than an hippopotamus and tusked. Because its name means "water lion" it may be a felid, but it would be unwise to state this with certainty.

COLEMAN FROG *Add to Dictionary article:* An examination has now revealed that this is a fake.

COLONIA ELIA CREATURE A humanoid with yellow hair reported in 2004 from this area of Argentina. It left large footprints. Its hands were clawlike. [#9 2]

COLORADO DINOSAUR A creature resembling a velociraptor which was reported to have crossed a street in Colorado in 2004. [120]

COLOURED RABBIT A kind of rabbit reported from the northerly regions of Scotland. Some specimens are ginger, some orange, some pink. Sightings have continued since the 1970s and their origin is a mystery. [#9]

COLUMBUS MOTHMAN A creature which attacked persons in the forest at Columbus (Ohio) in 2003. It was grey and screeched. [174]

CONVERSE SWAMP MONSTER This swamp near Converse (Indiana) was where a monster was allegedly heard in 1904. A woman gathering berries claimed to have seen a big black object which was thought to be the creature. [12]

COSTA RICAN CREATURE A black unidentified animal, bipedal with a long tail and tongue, 40cm in height, which was disturbed killing hens at night at San Juan de San Ramon in March, 2004. [1]

COTENTIN CREATURE Black, dolphin-snouted creature seen off the French coast in 1970. [155]

COUPAN Term applied to the so-called "Cordering Cougar", a mystery black felid of Australia.

CROOKED ISLAND SNAKE Two specimens of this snake were killed on Crooked Island in the Bahamas by the Columbus expedition in 1492. Their description does not tally with that of any known snake in the Bahamas and their identity remains a mystery. [#7]

CUBAN PTERODACTYL A pair of these was reported and sketched in 1971. [2]

CURDRIDGE SEA SERPENT A photograph, now apparently in a pub in Curdridge (Hants), has been taken of a 15-20' sea-serpent allegedly captured in a nearby river in the early 20th Century. [85]

CURELOMS AND CUMOMS The Book of Mormon is regarded as veridical scripture by the Church of Jesus Christ of Latter-Day Saints. It was translated, they maintain, from golden plates by their prophet, Joseph Smith. It contains the names of two mystery animals, cureloms and cumoms, and speculation has arisen as to what they are supposed to be. It says they were used by the Jaredites, who had migrated to

America after the attempted building of the Tower of Babel. They are domesticated creatures mentioned in Ether 9:19 and are described as useful. While many non-Mormons would simply regard the words as concoctions of Smith, Mormons have guessed that they were in fact mammoths, mastodons, tapirs, jaguars, llamas, giant sloths or unknown animals. (I am not sure how jaguars might be counted as useful. Perhaps they're good for keeping the mice down).

DANUBE MONSTER There have been reports of a monster in this river, a number from the town of Novi Sad (Serbia). A teacher of Russian named M. Pejin claimed to have seen a smooth-skinned , fast-swimming monster in 1980. He saw at least 2m of the body. It did not look like a large fish such as the catfish. There were other reports in 1997. *See also* **Danube Serpent.** [155]

DANUBE SERPENT Gigantic serpents are supposed to grace this river. [155]

DARK-COLOURED FISH An unknown piscid with a white "body" (?underbelly), a thin tail and spikes seen on Thor Heyerdahl's *Kon-Tiki* expedition in 1947. [C/H]

DARK WINGED BEAST This has been reported from Lobos (California).

DARLINGTON WINGED REPTILE This creature, 15' in length, was reported from Darlington County (South Carolina) in 1888. [N]

DARUC Term for a wildman used in Hautes-Alpes, France. [183]

DE'LYE'D A headless creature in Navaho myth, it nonetheless boasted four horns. He was sometimes thought of as a gigantic gopher. [R8]

DEMON OCTOPUS Dangerous fish supposed to live off the Marquesas Islands. It is huge in size. [10]

DENSMORE HILL MONSTER A creature supposed to lurk near Hartland (Vermont). There have been reports of it since 1763, but what it is actually supposed to look like is difficult to determine. [N]

DERIDDER ROADKILL A dead animal which was photographed in 1966 near Deridder (Louisiana). It cannot be identified with certainty and may be an unknown animal. It has even been suggested that it is a dead chupacabras. [120]

DERRYLEA LOUGH MONSTER The creature concerned, a water monster, was seen on land in the vicinity of this Irish lough by one Matty McDonagh. It jumped onto a wall. [143]

DEVASTATING DOG These dogs are said to be fierce canids found on Tonga and in Hawaii. They are said to eat children. [G10]

DEVIL'S POINT CREATURE A strange creature hooked by angler Nic Johnson at this location near Plymouth in 1987. It was (thought the witness) about twice the size of a horse, had menacing jaws, the eyes were frontal, the head covered with skin that resembled green-brown fur. There were no visible ears, but it was definitely not a seal. It may have been pursuing conger eels, known to frequent the Devil's Point area. [#1]

DIABLITO 20" humanoid reported from Pitrufquen, Argentina, in 2001-2002. [N]

DIFFERENT-FOOTED FOWL This bird was supposed to have one webbed foot (for swimming) and one clawed foot (for catching fish). It was noted as far apart as Florida (in 1519) and Canada. [H17]

DINOSAUR KANGAROO These creatures, 2m tall, were reported by motorists in the Atacama Desert, Chile, in 2004.   [1]

DIPLOCAULUS An amphibian that supposedly became extinct 270 million years ago. A photograph of a supposedly recently seen one has been circulating, but it may well be a hoax. Indeed, at least one person has claimed to be the hoaxer.

DISMAL SWAMP FREAK Folklorist David Barefoot regales us with the history of this hairy humanoid of North Carolina, which may have been of the Bigfoot variety. Caught and caged, it pined to death.

DOCAT The hybrid of a dog and a cat. A well-known American tabloid newspaper has asserted that these not only exist, but are on the prowl in the United States. I surmise zoologists would argue that such a hybrid is absolutely impossible. In fact, I feel they would do more than argue, they would issue a categorical and dismissive statement.

DOG-FACED KANGAROO-LIKE CREATURES Near Arica (Chile), the Abett de la Torre Diaz family, out driving at night, encountered dog-faced kangaroo-like beings which could fly. This occurred in 2004. [28]

DOG-FACED WINGED CREATURE Two specimens of this animal, a large and a small creature, were reported to have attacked one Juan Acuna in Chile in 2004. They showed astonishing strength. Local official Ricardo Encina said that the witness's wounds were genuine.   [1]

DOG-PORCUPINE CREATURE Seen in January, 2005, in Brigham City (Utah), this creature looked like a dog covered in hard, black, 3" long quills. The quills were clearly growing from the creature and not implanted by an attacking porcupine. [2]

DOG-TAILED MEN According to Cusick's *History of the Six Nations* (1823), a nation of humans with dogs' tails, discovered by a prehistoric Iroquois expedition.

DOMAIN CREATURE The Domain park in Auckland, New Zealand, seems to be the habitat of an unknown nocturnal creature which leaves traces in the form of large footprints and droppings, the latter belonging to no known animal. That it is an herbivore is indicated by scratches it leaves on trees. [1]

DORSET MYSTERY SNAKE An anomalous snake encountered by a man named

Dunford in Dorset. The date of the encounter is unknown, though likely to have been in the 1920s. The reptile was perhaps 6' long with a zigzag pattern on its back.

DOWA BEAST *Add to Dictionary article:* It was supposed to have been killed and identified as a female spotted hyena, but some doubt exists over the identification. [85]

DOWN HUMANOID A creature reported from Co Down (Ireland). It is 8' tall and has red eyes. [85]

DOX The supposed hybrid of a dog and a fox. It is doubtful that one has ever really existed. One alleged dox died without being scientifically examined.

DUAH *Add to Dictionary article:* The correct form of this word may be *duwas* and it may be identical with the ropen.

DUBAI RED-BACKED SPIDER The Australian red-backed spider (*Latrodectus hasselti*) has now been found in Dubai, United Arab Emirates, where a population may have established itself. [1]

DULVERTON PRIMATE A silver-coated gorilla-like primate 2.5m tall which chased a couple near Lake Dulverton (Tasmania) in 1967. This does not seem consistent, insofar as colour goes, with the usual descriptions of yowies. Although there may have been other sightings, local opinion tended to be sceptical about the incident.

DUNGARVON WHOOPER A mystery creature of New Brunswick, known only from the eerie sounds it makes. [N]

DWARF SEAL A kind of seal in Eskimo lore, said to be found in Willerstedt Lake, Victoria Island, Canada. [A5]

DYIRRI-DYIRRITCH A kind of wildman with a taste for human flesh in Australian Aboriginal lore. It was intelligent enough to make spears. [G11]

DZAGIN EMGEN A female almas. [183]

EAST INDIES MANTA RAY A huge and unidentified ray discovered in 1682. It had seven spines in its tail, which other manta rays lack. It took fourteen zebus to pull it ashore. [C/H]

EAST KILBRIDE HUMANOID Around East Kilbride (Scotland) there have recently been reports of a humanoid with bulbous eyes, blue skin and yellow patches on his legs and throat. There has been a suggestion that genetic engineering has been involved. [85]

EBU GOGO *see* **Homo floresiensis.**

ECKANDER CREATURE A woman perceived a creature that looked like a stick man as she approached her farmhouse door at night time. It turned its head and looked at her. This occurred in 2004 at Eckander (Iowa). [1]

EGG PEOPLE Name given to BHMs which have been observed searching for food in the Perdue Egg Dump (Maryland). [183]

EKUNEIL A huge snake in Aztec lore with a tendency to suck its victims' blood. [G10]

EL CAMPO APE MAN A 5' tall creature, greyish in colour, with simian characteristics, reported in this Texas locale in 2004. [120]

ELMENDORF BEAST A strange creature shot by a farmer in Texas in 2004. Though identified as a mange-ridden coyote, there are indications that it was nothing of the sort. To confuse matters, some customer at Delcon's Grocery and Market in Elmendorf identified it from a photograph as a chupacabras, to which it bears not the slightest resemblance. The animal looks canine and is blue and hairless. Similar animals have been reported for a number of years. Even a hairless blue mother with hairless blue cubs has been reported. Author Whitley Streiber has managed to procure a photograph of a specimen. The animal's movements are unlike those of a coyote. All this would indicate that it is an unrecognised species.

O. Bracken claimed to have seen a blue/grey beast of this nature whose coat later changed to tan/red. [#9]

ELWEDRITSCHE A legendary creature of the Rhineland region which looks like a chicken with antlers. [182]

ENCANTADO Encantados are the were-dolphins of Brazil. They are dolphins that assume human form. In this guise, they can often play the saxophone. No social opprobrium attends a girl becoming pregnant by an encantado. [H16]

ERITREAN CANID An unknown member of the dog family which has been seen in the Danakil Depression of Eritrea. [2]

ETCHEMIN RIVER MONSTER In the legends of the Abenaki Indians, this Quebecois river was and possibly still is tenanted by a monster. [N]

ETHIOPIAN ANT A creature of classical lore, said to be the size of a dog and to have a taste for human flesh. [120]

EVERGLADES APE Alternative name for the skunk ape.

EZITAPILE EXOTIC This creature is reputed to have a horse-like head and mane, a barrel-like torso and a snakelike body. It is coloured yellow and appears to live in the forest in South Africa, from where it has been reported. [N]

FALSE POTTO Skeletons collected in Cameroon, though apparently of pottos, showed in two instances tails, which pottos are not supposed to have. This has led some scientists to suggest that we have here an unknown species which they have labelled Martin's False Potto (*Pseudopotto martini*). Not all zoologists agree that they represent an hitherto unknown species.

FANAMPITOLOHO A seven-headed monstrous creature in the lore of Madagascar. [179]

FAVIA Diminutive humanoids who, in French folklore, lived in the Cote Rousse Forest. They had a tendency to pillage human garments, presumably when they were hanging on clotheslines. They were coloured white. [183]

FIELD FOX A sort of werefox in Japanese lore. They can transform themselves into humans or something inanimate. They live out in fields. [H16]

FIERY VIPER A kind of viper once supposed to have been found in Wales. There were never more than two of these creatures, a male and female, for when they became parents, they would be eaten by their young. [T3]

FINIST This legendary Russian bird seems to be based ultimately on the phoenix. It is a hawk by day, a young man by night.

FINMAN A kind of merbeing in Scottish belief. They try to capture fishermen as husbands for their finwomen, who will not lose their looks if they marry a human. [*Scotsman* website]

FIREMAN The name given to a rumoured New Zealand bird, a variety of kiwi. [179]

FISH LAKE WILD CHILD Michigan City (Indiana) was the place where a (?humanoid) "wild child" was reported in the vicinity of Fish Lake in 1839. [R4]

FISH-MAN This creature was of humanoid shape, with anatine feet and a tail. It was killed at Exeter in 1737. [146]

FITTLEWORTH DRAGON A monster reported a number of times near Fittleworth (Sussex) in the 19th Century. It would spit at humans, but not attack them. At the time, people were convinced it was a dinosaur. It was last seen in 1867. [1]

FLAT ROCK SNAKE A giant snake reported from a river near Flat Rock (Indiana) in 1946. It was estimated at 20' in length. Trails suggested it had made its way into the town of Flat Rock itself. [R6]

FLINT MAN A living monster rock in Jicarillo Apache legend. It was killed by Killer of Enemies. [L5]

FLORIDA MYSTERY BIRD This bird could not be identified by the witnesses, who were sure it was not an eagle, owl or vulture. It had, however, a vulturine beak, a white streak at the back of the head and was 3-4' tall, with a 6' wingspan. [162]

FLORIDA SQUID An unknown kind of squid seen by scientists using a Deep Sea

Eye off the Florida coast. The sighting was reported in 2005. The investigating scientists were from the Harbor Branch Oceanographic Institute. [120]

FLYING CREATURE A creature with a large wingspan (estimated at from 10-20') seen by three witnesses in Sutherland, Scotland, in 1993. It was seen after nightfall and seemed too slow to be an eagle. None of the witnesses could identify it.   [2]

FLYING SERPENT This was seen from a Missouri steamboat in 1857. [N]

FOX-SIZED CAT These wild animals, which may be true wildcats rather than ferals, were reported in H. Bourne *Living on Exmoor* (1963). They were also said to be found in Exeter until the 1970s. [1]

FRENCH FLYING SNAKE A green flying snake was reported in the Alpes-Maritimes area of France in 1930 or 1931.

FRIAS HUMANOID An Argentinian policeman in 2000 mistook this for a child, but it turned out to be a menacing humanoid. [187]

FRIGHTFUL INSECT An insect so described was supposedly hatched in the cheekbone of Ann Liddell, who dwelt in Carlisle in the 18th Century. [J1]

FUNKWE A monster looking like a snake which local lore placed in Lake Chilengwa, Zambia.

GAHANNA LION In 2004 in Gahanna, a suburb of Columbus (Ohio), sundry reports came in of a lion in the area.

GAMMONS LANE BIRD Large bird, 6' tall at least, with black fur on its head, reported by A. Driscoll, who claims he saw it in Watford, England, about 1980, when he was a child. [2]

GANI An Iranian dragon. [186]

GAS STREET EEL Huge black eel said to have been seen in the Gas Street Canal, Birmingham. [N]

GATINEAU RIVER MONSTER An unidentified creature with a head like that of a horse has been reported in this Canadian river.

GEORGIA MYSTERY CAT Unidentified felid said to be 2'6"-3' tall and 4-5'6" long. It has been reported from Georgia, USA. It looks like a domestic cat, but its ears resemble a bobcat's. Its tail, on the other hand, is very different from the tail of that well known animal.. It was observed in 2004. [153]

GERMAN SIMIAN I have so described these two animals as it seems uncertain whether they were apes or monkeys. Their provenance is a mystery. They were seen in Mecklenburg-Vorpommern, in the north of Germany, in 1938.

GHINDARING Red-haired humanoid in Australian Aboriginal legend. [G11]

GHOST HORSE OF THE PRAIRIE Some said it was white, some silver grey, some steel-blue. It is the subject of a widespread legend in the American West. Washington Irving saw it in Oklahoma in 1832. [H17]

GIANT CANADIAN FISH A huge fish which was apparently to be found in Les Trois Lacs (Quebec) until the middle of the 20th Century. [M7]

GIANT CRUSTACEAN This was seen by a 13-year old girl at Ladies Cove, West Kirby, and later by fishermen. It was grey and had 4-6 jointed legs. [2]

GIANT EVERGLADES SNAKE In the lore of the Seminole Indians, such snakes, evidently pythons, exist or existed. [A5]

GIANT HARE This startling lagomorph was observed in Ireland about 1947. The witness said it was the size of a large dog. [N]

GIANT LIGURIAN FISH Seen off the Ligurian Riviera (N.W. Italy), this large fish or cetacean was found dying. It was brought ashore, but experts couldn't identify it. [155]

GIANT LIZARD (ETHIOPIAN) Such a beast, 10-12' long with a dorsal crest, has been reported.

GIANT MOUSE At the close of the Middle Ages, such rodents were said by Europeans to be found in India, in size as great as cats. [B19]

GIANT ORANG-UTAN Very large specimens of this ape, perhaps constituting a discrete species, have been encountered. [A5]

GIANT OZARK CENTIPEDE It is rumoured that, in the Ozarks, you can find centipedes as long as 18". Although these creatures seem to be quite well known, they appear to have never been catalogued by science. [2]

GIANT OZARK FROG Apparently such frogs are to be found in the folklore of the Ozarks. [2]

GIANT PIKE Such a creature, 6' long, is reported from Lake Remi (Quebec). [M7]

GIANT RABBIT *Add to Dictionary article:* Giant rabbits in England have been reported from Hampshire and Surrey.

GIANT RAY Such a creature was reported from Lake Gutierrez (Argentina) in 1976. Rays are supposed to be found only at sea. [N]

GIANT SALMON Irish tradition states such a creature was caught at Clonmacnoise in 1113. [#9]

GIANT SARDINIAN LIZARD An unknown reptile reported from this Italian island. [155]

GIANT TIGER Large tigers with an extra toe per foot, reputedly friendly to humans, have been reported from China. [2]

GIANT TURKISH SNAKE This was about 3.5m long and was about in 1938, in the region of Balikessir. It was eventually killed by a forester. [155]

GIANT UKRAINIAN SPIDER A rumour on the Internet and in the Press claims that a giant spider the size of a Jack Russell terrier had been hiding in a lift shaft . This creature, it is stated, was responsible for the death of a postman, a child and a sergeant. Russian authorities eventually destroyed it and discovered a great quantity of its eggs. [S19]

GIANT VAMPIRE-BAT This creature is sometimes reported from the south-east of Brazil. [168]

GIANT WOLVERINE A huge wolverine in the belief of the Athabascan Indians of Canada, it will at times emerge from its forested lair to scoff an unhappy human. [G10]

GIGANTIC OCTOPUS *Add to Dictionary article:* DNA evidence has established that the Giant Octopus of St Augustine (Florida) was a decomposing whale.

GLENDARRY LAKE MONSTER Observed on the banks of this Irish lake, this monster hopped. Its head was compared with a sheep's and its neck was long. It was also seen in the lake itself and may have been scaly. [146]

GLENELG MONSTER This Scottish monster was seen in 1872 in the water between Glenelg and Lochourn. It had humps and was coloured black. [146]

GODZILLA Are you familiar with the gigantic lizard of the Japanese screen? Good, because conspiracy rumour is now saying certain Japanese are actually breeding these creatures and 450 of them are in existence. The intention, it is averred, is to get them to revenge Hiroshima. Does this mean they'll be taught to fly aeroplanes? However, you never know. Perhaps they'll be of amicable disposition.

GOLDEN RAT OF KENWOOD A mysterious animal spotted in the London area in 2004. It was described by witness Karen Stoker as bigger than a rat and smaller than a fox. She saw it swimming and discerned no tail. Other pedestrians have seen it. [2]

GOLSPIE SEA SERPENT A brown and yellow creature seen off the Scottish coast in the 1870s. [146]

GRAHAMSTOWN MYSTERY CAT In the 19th Century two specimens of a mystery cat were killed near Grahamstown, South Africa.. It had small spots, but these were joined along the back, making this part of the creature black. The specimens' shoulders were of an orange colour, while the rest of the pelage was tawny. [153]

GRAND LAKE MONSTER Towards the end of the 1960s a monster was reported in this New Brunswick lake. [E]

GRANDMOTHER SPIDER Huge and dangerous spider said to be found in the Rocky Mountains. [A4]

GREAT MOOSE A large kind of creature, said to dwarf all lesser mooses, with an extra leg sticking out of its shoulder with which to prepare its bed. Its skin was impervious to arrows or bullets. The writer of this description in 1666 said there had recently been an unsuccessful hunt for it. [H17]

GREAT NAKED BEAR A fierce beast in the lore of the Native Americans. C. De Voe says this legend is one of the oldest Delaware stories. However, it is not confined to that nation. This animal is said to have a white, hairy spot on its back, but to be otherwise hairless. It was much larger than an ordinary bear. Difficult to kill, often the only way to slay it was by breaking its backbone. An early account of the beast was written by J. Hackewelder in 1797. The Indians gave him to understand the creature was extinct. Indian mothers frightened their children by telling them the naked bear would eat them if they were disobedient. [A5 D11]

GREAT SLAVE LAKE MONSTER A large and speedy monster has been reported in this Canadian lake. It seems to be green in colour. One description mentions a draconic head, another considers the head like that of a pike. It has been said that its body is like an alligator's. Apart from modern sightings, it was known in Dene Indian tradition. It is said to live off Utsingh Point. [1]

GREEN MAN A humanoid of Pennsylvania which, it is said, will approach your car and gaze in through the windows. [A4]

GREEN SWAMP CREATURE This creature was observed in Polk County (Florida) in 2004 by Jennifer Ward in the Green Swamp. It looked human, its eyes were encircled by white rings and it had dark hair or fur. [2]

GREY CREATURE Looking like a snake and moving like a caterpillar, this creature was seen crossing the A85 in Scotland in 1965 by two motorists. Its length was estimated at 6m. [146]

GRIFFIN *Add to Dictionary article:* In Berber belief, the griffin has the head of an eagle and the body of a fox or wolf. It is the result of crossbreeding. [K5]

GUNNI A wombat-like creature of Australian folklore. It is said to have something resembling horns or antlers on its head. There was a recent sighting in 1999 in Victoria. The suspicion seems to exist that the gunni, like the drop bear, is a possible hoax creature. [N]

HAAST'S EAGLE A New Zealand bird (*Harpagornis moorei*) which is said to have become extinct four hundred years ago, but there have been some possible modern sightings.

HAIRY MAN Alaskan term for a BHM.

HALF KANGAROO A creature that looked like half a man, half a kangaroo was the perpetrator of an attack in Fremantle (Western Australia), the port of Perth. I have not been able to discover the date of this incident or, indeed, which half of the creature resembled a man and which half a kangaroo. [85]

HAMEH In the legendry of Arabia, a bird which springs from the blood of a murder victim. [26]

HANG HAU FELID A large black/grey cat reported from this area of Hong Kong in 1976. It killed twenty dogs. [N]

HAPAI-CAN In Aztec lore, a child-devouring serpent. [G10]

HARFORD SNAKE A giant serpent, it was 20' long and its thickness was compared with that of a man's body. It was seen by a number of people in Harford County (Maryland) in 1875. [R6]

HARTSVILLE SNAKE A 20' long giant snake coloured a bright brown and black seen in 1991 near Hartsville (Tennessee). [R6]

HATTON CAT Unidentified rusty brown ABC seen in Scotland in 2002. [167]

HATUIBWARI In Melanesian myth, a creature with the upper part of its body human, the rest like a winged snake. This creature is supposed to be the ancestor of humanity. [160]

HAVALO BAY CREATURE There was a US base here on Florida Island, near Guadalcanal, Solomon Islands. One night, as the servicemen were watching a film, some creature got in and ran amok among them, crushing the legs of some. This animal could not be made out in the dark. The uninjured made a beeline for the security of their tents. One opinion was that the creature had come out of the sea. [85]

HAWAIIAN SEA SERPENT A creature seen and photographed by E. Ushio off Hawaii in 2004. He speculated that it might be a periscope rather than an animal, but this is far from certain. [34]

HAZEL SNAKE Estimated at 28' in length, this giant snake was seen near Hazel (Kentucky) in 1962. [R6]

HEAVENLY HORSE Mythical horse that may have a basis in reality, once existing on the Sino-Siberian border.

HELENSBURGH CREATURE A lengthy creature seen at the mouth of the Clyde (in Scotland) in 1962. It left large footprints. [146]

HELL'S GATE SEA SERPENT A sea serpent which attacked a ship off the New York coast in 1902, ramming it twice. [N]

HELOHA According to the Choctaw, a female thunderbird. [186]

HERRING HOGG According to the folklore of Cheshire, a horrid and noisy beast which emerged from the sea at Wirral in 1636. No one would approach it until it had died. [N]

HIGHWAY 13 REPTILE MAN Winged reptoid said to have been seen in Wisconsin some years ago.

HIPPOCAMPUS Alternative name for the mythological and also the zoological sea horse. *See* **Sea Horse** in *Dictionary.*

HIRCOCERVUS A creature combining elements of goat and deer.

HIYITL'IIK A serpentine beast in the lore of the Manhousat Indians of Vancouver Island. It is 7-8' long and can travel on land as well as in the water. It was also credited with the ability to grow wings. [1]

HOADE MONSTER A carcass discovered at Bungle Creek, Australia, by a man named Hoade in 1883. It was 30' long with a trunk but no head and something like a lobster's tail. Charles Fort mentioned the possibility of its having been teleported to earth from the moon or Mars. [120]

HOCKOMOCK SNAKE A giant snake reported by a number of witnesses in 1939 in a Massachussetts swamp. [R6]

HOG MOUNTAIN CAT A mystery felid, compared in size to a golden retriever, orange in colour, spotted in Gwinnett County (Ga.). [153]

HOLLYWOOD MOTHMAN The Hollywood concerned is in Maryland. This creature was seen in 1944 and was of huge size. It was descried landing after nightfall and walking off into the distance. [R6]

HOLOPAW GORILLA Humanoid reported from Florida. [179]

HOMBRE DE LAS MONTANAS A BHM supposed to inhabit Ecuador. There was a sighting in 1985. [183]

HOMME DE BOUC French term for a Wildman.

HOMO FLORESIENSIS A hominid whose remains were discovered on the island of Flores (Indonesia) in 2004 and first reported in the journal *Nature.* Said remains were of at least seven creatures. They were over 3' in height, existed until 13,000 years ago and may even exist today, as local tradition speaks of a legendary race of small people called the Ebu Gogo. These had been an omnivorous little people who could repeat human sentences and had a language of their own. When they stole and ate a baby, locals set fire to their cave, but a couple escaped. One report said one had been seen recently. These are said in the case of females, to have long breasts which they throw over their shoulders. They are never associated with stone tools, however, while *Homo floresiensis* was acquainted with them. *Homo floresiensis* may have used stone tools, but their brains were very small. They are thought to be descended from *Homo erectus*, though variant opinion regards them as merely a subspecies of *Homo sapiens*. An argument that they are merely microcephalic children of modern humans can hardly be sustained. An independent team led by Dr D Fall (Florida State University) has identified the creature as a new species. Their findings are published in *Science*, but some controversy remains.

HOOP SNAKE Snake in American folklore that rolls along, holding its tail in its mouth. In 1925 the magazine *Natural History* described it as a myth. However, Leon Hale of the *Houston Chronicle* has received many reports of the creature, though none of recent sightings. Snakes which behave similarly are not unknown in Scandinavian legend.

HOOTER Name for a BHM in Indiana. [183]

HORNED SERPENT According to Cusick's *History of the Six Nations* (1828), this creature came to the surface of Lake Ontario 2200 years before the arrival of Columbus in America (1492). Its smell was so appalling it killed a number of people.

HORNED SNAKE Snakes with two horns apiece and with bright, glittering skin were to be found long ago, according to the Cherokee. [169]

HOROMATANGI Lake-dwelling monsters of Maori lore, said to combine elements of human and reptile. They are said to have a taste for human flesh. [G10]

HORROR OF HAMPSHIRE Emily Parkinson looked out of her window at 11 o'clock at night on 21st February, 2004. She was horrified to see on the lawn a humanoid with an eye situated in its stomach. She was also conscious of a noise which seemed to affect her mind. She had been awoken by a light. [A4]

HORSE OF HILLAROO A winged horse in the folklore of the Orkney Islands. It is said to carry off children. [A4]

HORSESHOE POND MONSTER Seen by a farmer in 1892, this creature was described as serpentine with a dog's head. Its back and sides were black. [#19]

HOVINGHAM CAT A big cat the size of a Labrador seen in Yorkshire in 1997. It was coloured white. [184]

HSIGO Winged human-faced monkey of Chinese lore. [26]

HUANG YAO The head of this creature resembles a cat's, the body is musteline. It is yellow and allegedly found in China. [E]

HUGE MASS A huge dark mass seen in the sea by the *Kon-Tiki* expedition of 1947. Though it was unidentified, Thor Heyerdahl thought it was some kind of ray. [C/H]

HUMAN-BEAR HYBRID According to legend, Siward, Earl of Huntingdon and Northumberland, who hailed originally from Denmark, who flourished in the reign of Edward the Confessor (1042-1066) and who features in Shakespeare's *Macbeth*, was the son of a human-bear hybrid, who resembled a human, but had a bear's ears. This person was the result of his mother's being raped by a bear. [H15]

HUMAN-ELEPHANT HYBRID The Indhlovu clan of the Zulus, whence sprang their greatest chiefs, claimed descent from such hybrids. The story starts with a rather plump Zulu woman who encountered a friendly and courteous elephant. [K5]

HUMAN-GORILLA HYBRID It is believed in part of Africa that there is a race of such hybrids which pose a danger to certain young women. Their fathers had married female gorillas, thinking they were beautiful women. The sooner they get more opticians out there, the better. A Russian doctor made the claim that human-gorilla hybrids had been bred in the USSR. [K5]

HUMAN-LION HYBRID These are said to be found in Sudan, where hunters are said to have relations with lionesses, a somewhat unsafe procedure at the best of times. These produce offspring who sometimes grow into beautiful young women, but, should you marry one, there is always the possibility she will eat you. [K5]

HUMAN-YETI HYBRID *Add to Dictionary article:* Near Dhading, Nepal, is supposed to live a population of mixed human/yeti descent. According to the story, in 1917 a boy was captured by a female yeti and these are their descendants.

HUMILITY Bird of North America, perennially in the air, never alighting. However, it can speak one word, "Humility". We are informed of this in S. Peters *General History of Connecticut* (1781).

HUNTLY CAT Unidentified white ABC seen in Aberdeenshire in 2001. [167]

HURACAN Term used for a dragon in the Caribbean. Here, dragons are supposed to cause hurricanes.

HYOTE Mystery creature of Baltimore County (Maryland). It was seen in 2004. A captured red fox with sarcoptic mange may have been the animal concerned. [152]

IDANHA-A-NOVA PREDATOR Mystery predator of Portugal, which has been draining the blood of sheep, puncturing their necks. While there was speculation that the chupacabras had reached Lusitanian shores, a zoological expert felt sure the culprit was a wolf.

IGUANA MEN Reptoids which came from the sky in Mayan tradition.

IKAL Diminutive humanoids of dwarfs in the beliefs of the Tzeltal, they are said to live underground and whose faces have been blackened by the sun.

ILIMU According to Kenyan tradition, an animal that likes to eat people and can change itself into human form. It does not seem to be necessarily any specific species of animal.

ILLANKANPANKA Name for an apelike creature in Queensland lore, perhaps identical with the jogung.

IMPUNDULU A large bird, sometimes of the vulture kind, which has commerce with women in African belief. The offspring of such unions are vampires. [K5]

INDIANAPOLIS CREATURE A creature with a baboon-like body and an orange head which somewhat resembled that of a dog, seen about 1980 in an Indianapolis suburb. The witness, who sent a communication to the Yahoo Cryptozoo group, thought it might have been a genetic experiment.

INGRAM VALLEY HOMINOID A hominoid reported from this Northumberland area without further data. [1]

INSTOW SERPENT A many-finned serpent seen in the water between Instow (Devon) and Bideford Bay in 1911. [146]

INVISIBLE FISH There is supposed to be a fish able to turn itself invisible off the Seychelles. If you cannot see it, it doesn't necessarily mean you need glasses.

IQALUAQPAK A water-monster with man-eating tendencies said by the Eskimo to inhabit McAlpine Lake in northern Canada. [G10]

ISCHAGGATTA Wildmen of Swiss tradition. [183]

ISCHIA SEA SERPENT It was seen off this Italian island in 1934. It was said to be in the region of 35' in length. [155]

ISIQUQUMADEVA Sauropod-like animal of central Africa. It is supposed to be saurian and long-necked, having legs like an elephant's and a long tail. [41]

ITALIAN MYSTERY FISH A large fish with a red head and a bluish tail was captured off the Ligurian coast in 1963. It was not identified. [155]

ITALIAN WILDMAN *Add to Dictionary article:* In Italian legends, wildmen were said to be found in both the Alps and the Appenines and humans sometimes employed them as herdsmen. They were knowledgeable about dairy products. They were generally not dangerous. An elderly Piedmontese said wildmen, though of solitary bent, were once a numerous race. Modern sightings include one in 1974 by an old woman, at the end of 1980 one was seen a number of times in the vicinity of the River Sale and in 1997 a sighting was reported in Grimaldi. [155]

ITOSHI A monster said to be found in the Kafue River, Zambia. It is said to be 50' in length.

IVORY-BILLED WOODPECKER *Add to Dictionary article:* In 2005, living specimens were allegedly discovered in Arkansas. The evidence is photographic and some doubts about it have been expressed by persons at Florida Gulf Coast University. [2]

JOGUNG A 7-10' tall creature, looking like a large ape, reported from Australia. These creatures are said to carry clubs. The *lo-an*, termed in the *Dictionary* a possible alternative name for the yowie, may in fact be a jogung.

JUPITER INLET CREATURE Near the end of the 19th Century, this strange creature was discerned at this Florida locale by Emily L. Bell and her husband. It was 30' long, its face was reminiscent of a human's, it reared up and then entered the sea. The impression given is it was somewhat serpentine. It turned out to be known to locals. [1]

KAHA Legendary bird of Tajikistan. Its blood is said to cure blindness. [N]

KALLANA A kind of pygmy elephant which the Kani tribe of the Agasthyavanam Forest (Kerala), India, claim exists. [158]

KANGAROO-LIKE BEAST Although this creature looked like a kangaroo, it clearly wasn't one, as it attacked and ate animals, while kangaroos are vegetarians. It was in the vicinity of South Pittsburg (Tennessee) in 1934.

KANSAI LAKE MONSTER Monsters are supposed to live in this Chinese lake and not to be above devouring animals on the shore.

KARKADANN An unicorn of Arabian tradition. Its horn was said to give protection against the scorpion. Its shape was not always certain, but it was believed to bear a general resemblance to an antelope. Killing a karkadann was deemed impossible, yet in one story four heroes did it. It eventually became confused with the rhinoceros. [L1/A]

KASHE HOTAHPALA Legendary creature of Mississippi, with upper parts human, lower parts like a deer and a scary visage. It is noted for its loud screams. While it likes to frighten people, it does them no harm. [183]

KELA-KEMBE This seems to be the name in the language of the Baka, a tribe of pygmies, for mokele-mbembe.

KENT MONSTER A strange monster was struck by lightning at Maidstone in 1205, according to a chronicle written five years later by Ralph of Essex.

KENTHURST CAT Mystery catlike animal which attacked Luke Walker (17) at Kenthurst Valley (New South Wales). Rex Gilroy thought it might be, not a cat, but a subspecies of thylacoleo, the supposedly extinct catlike Australian marsupial. Mayor Stubbs of Hawkesbury expressed concern. It has now been suggested there is a family group in the area.

KESHENA LAKE SNAKE A creature with horns which inhabits this Wisconsin lake in Indian lore.

KETTHONTLA A creature of Orkney folklore, but no tradition remains concerning her appearance. Speculation suggests she was a mixture of cat and dog. [159]

KHI-TRAU Humanoid creature of the borderlands of laos. [183]

KILTANYA Wildman with protruberant eyes reported from Siberia.

KILWA CREATURE A reportedly peculiar creature captured in the sea off Kilwa, Tanzania, around 1975. It looked like a fish, had arms and legs, had two eyes, one glowing, and a horn. [#9]

KITSUNE *Add to Dictionary article:* There are four kinds, each having different powers – byakko, koko, jenko and reiko.

KNOCK FOREST HUMANOID A humanoid that ran at about 70 m.p.h. reported from this part of Lothian. It was supposedly seen by a family. [146]

KNOX COUNTY CAT An ABC active in Knox County (Indiana) in 1908. It was first said to be in the region of Pike and Gibson, later upping stakes and moving to Snyder's Gulch.

KNOX COUNTY CREATURE A beast with a 4' stride whose trail began in a landfill site in Knox County (Indiana) and which showed the beast was able to force its way through thick woodland. The creature was never identified. [#19]

KOH-MEH-COH-GOH-YOSE Hirsute diminutive beings of Puerto Rico. In the 1980s one fell in love with a Protestant minister, which afforded him much consternation. When it entered his church and tried to drag him forth, the congregation fled, thinking it was the devil. [183]

KOREAN TIGER Tigers are supposed to be extinct in Korea, but there is some evidence that this supposition is premature.

KORESEK Kind of kangaroo in Iranian belief. [85]

KOSOVO WILDMAN This creature was reported near Kamenica. It had reddish hair, which was longer on the head than elsewhere. It was about 5'6" tall. The face was flat and black, the hands were also black. [2]

KRAITBULL A kind of apelike creature in Australian lore.

KREUTZET Gigantic bird which, Aldrovandus informs us, dwelt in Russia.

KUDLOOPUDLOOALUK A sea serpent in Eskimo lore, it will drag the unwary into the water. [G10]

KUN A monstrous fish of Chinese lore that could transform into a bird. [152]

KUNDUWA Legendary flying creature of New Guinea. [2]

KUNGSTORN Gigantic eagle of European folklore, this may have inspired some Big Bird reports if it in fact exists. The large bird that carried off Svanhild Hansen (aged 3) in 1932 and put her down again unharmed in Scandinavia was thought to be a kungstorn.

LA BELLE LAKE FISH Unidentified gigantic fish have been reported from this American lake. [C1]

LAKE ALBA CUYYA MONSTER A long-necked monster was reported from this lake in Victoria (Australia) in the 19th Century. [N]

LAKE BERGSJO MONSTER This Norwegian lake has been the locale of monster reports, the animal concerned having a 3' neck.

LAKE BILEC AMPHIBIAN A supposedly new kind of amphibian, reported from this lake in Bosnia-Herzegovina in 2004. [155]

LAKE BOROVACKO MONSTER Stories reporting a monster in this Serbian lake date from the 1990s. [155]

LAKE CHEHALIS MONSTER This lake lies in Washington state. The monster was said to have a snake's head and alligator's body. It had wings which appeared leathery. It attacked a swimmer, according to a report published in 1892. [R6]

LAKE COMO MONSTER Unidentified animals resembling reptiles have been reported from this Italian lake. This kind of creature is locally called *lariosauro*. A submarine manned by smugglers, captured in 1947, may have added to the legend. [155]

LAKE CONWAY CREATURE Various strange creatures have been indistinctly seen in this Arkansas lake. [N]

LAKE DEBLEMYREN MONSTER A serpentine monster with a mane was reported in this Norwegian lake in 1867. [32]

LAKE DE SMET MONSTER This Wyoming lake is said to be home to a number of monsters, a couple of which were observed in 1892. [N]

LAKE DEWEY PTEROSAUR A pterosaur was reported by a witness over this lake in 1969. [161]

LAKE DISTRICT FLYING CREATURE About 1997 this creature was made out after nightfall in the sky above Cumbria. It resembled a manta ray. It was seen by about ten people between Little Langdale and Coniston. According to legend, a similar creature had been seen on the ground by two climbers a couple of centuries previously. It had vanished on their approach. [2]

LAKE DOWNEY PARK CREATURE A strange bipedal figure with storklike legs which pursued a witness at Orlando (Florida) in February, 2004. [1]

LAKE ERIE MONSTER *Add to Dictionary article:* According to the *Leamington Post,* the first sighting was in 1792 near Snake Island. The Creation Evidence Museum of Glen Rose (Texas) houses a stuffed reptile 31" long found on the shores of Lake Erie which they assert to be a baby plesiosaur.

LAKE GARDA MONSTER A monster resembling a plesiosaur was reported from this Italian lake in 1965. [155]

LAKE GENEVA MONSTER There were early, but no recent, reports of a monster in this Swiss lake. [N]

LAKE ISHIKU MONSTER Vaguely attested monster in this Zambian lake.

LAKE KANIANKA MONSTER This Slovak lake is supposed to play home to a monster. [N]

LAKE MAGGIORE MONSTER This Italian lake is said to house a monster with a horselike head. [#9]

LAKE MIMINSKA MONSTER This Ontario lake was said to boast a monster or monsters. [N]

LAKE MURRAY MONSTER In 1995 a monster was observed to quit this lake in Papua-New Guinea and munch some vegetation. A resemblance to an iguanodon was remarked on. [N]

LAKE OSENSJOEN MONSTER According to Norwegian folklore, there is a monster in this lake. No one has reported seeing it in modern times. [N]

LAKE PALIC MONSTER This creature has been reported from Serbia recently. It is supposed to be a gigantic serpentine being with legs resembling a duck's. It is nicknamed *Mulijko* (muddy one). [155]

LAKE ST CLAIR MONSTER A mystery creature in this Ontario lake, described as looking like an eel, was reported to have killed a horse on the shore in 1897. [172]

LAKE SEMETES MONSTER A serpent-like monster with a dorsal fin has been reported from this Serbian lake. It is said to come ashore and bellow. [155]

LAKE SKODJE MONSTER This Norwegian lake monster is supposed to have a horse's head and to be 20' long. [32]

LAKE SNASA MONSTER There is said to be a monster in this Norwegian lake which sensibly surfaces only in calm weather. [C1]

LAKE SULDAL MONSTER Lake monster reported from Iceland. [179]

LAKE TINNSJON FISH Unknown kind of fish actually filmed in this Norwegian lake in 2004. The film was broadcast on Norwegian television.

LAKE TONI SNAKE A giant snake is reported, not to live in, but to burrow near, this Siberian lake. [#12]

LAKE VEDLOZERO CREATURE A mysterious creature that bore some resemblance to a human was reported in this lake in Karelia in 1928. [1]

LAMASSU Winged lion of Akkadian mythology.

LAN-JEN Dimnutive hairy humanoid used as an assistant by a hunter in Manchuria in 1914. [183]

LANCASHIRE SNAKE A strange reptile described in *The Diary of Samuel Pepys* (17th Century). Pepys himself did not see this creature, but was told of it. Apparently it had the power to place itself under a skylark and send poison shooting into the air, which struck the poor bird, which would then fall into the open mouth of the serpent below.

LAO CAI CIVET A kind of civet, perhaps an unknown species, reported from Vietnam.

LASCAUX BEAST An unknown animal amongst the famous cave paintings at Lascaux, dating from 17,000 years ago. It is sometimes called an unicorn, but in fact sports two horns. It is of a reddish colour with spots.

LAUGHING POPARINA Term used for a BHM in Maryland.

LEBANESE MOTHMAN   A creature reportedly sighted in Lebanon in 2004. [174]

LEGAROU Trinidadian term for a werewolf.

LEGGED SNAKE A 2' long snake with a pair of what were apparently small legs discovered in a garden in Richland (Washington) in 2005. [85]

LESSER SUNDAS CAT Name given by M. Newton to the cryptid listed in *Dictionary* as the Alor-Solor cat.

LEXINGTON CREATURE It had bluish-grey fur, black spots, long teeth and a snout and was seen near Lexington (Kentucky) in December, 2004. Its shoulder height was about 3' and its back, which boasted a fringe of fur, sloped downwards. The head was large. [2]

LICATA FISH Giant unidentified fish or possibly whale stranded at Licata (Sicily) in 1741. [N]

LICKING COUNTY LION Mysterious felid reported from Licking County (NY). Witnesses include a brace of police officers who called it a "cat-like animal". The creature was described as 2.5' wide and 6.5' long by witness Marc Trombino, who said it was like "a wolf on steroids".   [2]

LI'KELA-BEMBE A dinosaur-like creature with a long neck reported from Cameroon. It may be simply another name for the mokele-mbembe. [N]

LINH DUONG *Add to Dictionary article:* A number of commentators have argued that the evidence for this creature has been hoaxed, but this opinion is not universal.

LION-MAN A werelion in the legends of the Bozo of Mali. You can recognise a lion-man by the whiff of carrion about him and his nasal voice. Copper bullets will kill a lion-man. According to the Kabyl of Algeria, the first lion was a man of wild habits. [K5]

LITTLE ARMIER FISH Mystery fish 20' long reported from Malta in 2003. [N]

LIVORNO WHALE In 1881 an unidentified whale was cast up near the Italian port of Leghorn or Livorno. Its head was somewhat leonine and it may have lacked a tail. [155]

LIZARD GIRL Rumour in India has it that a girl has turned into a sort of half-lizard creature. Although her mother is said to have brought her to hospital, the story has not been substantiated. [120]

LLYN CAU MONSTER A monster reportedly inhabits this Welsh lake. It is supposed to have once drowned a man. [146]

LONG FISH An unknown eel-shaped creature, seen on the *Kon-Tiki* expedition in the Pacific in 1947. It had two dorsal fins, a tailfin shaped like a sickle and a slender snout. [C/H]

LORRAINE SEA SERPENT Marine animal espied in the North Atlantic from the *Lorraine* in 1904. It had horns and a single dorsal fin. Witnesses computed its length at 150'. The large size of its eyes also elicited comment.

LOUGH CLADDAGHDUFF MONSTER At first mistaken for a bullock, this creature turned out to look more like an eel. It had a white underside. It was observed in this Irish lough in 1956. [C1]

LOUP-GAROU The French term for a werewolf; cf. Medieval Latin *gerulfus.* However, the term has wider significance than its English counterpart, in that it can be applied to virtually any were-animal. In Haiti it can be applied to a were-plant. The loup-garou has found its way from France to Canada, where there is actually a Mount Loup-Garou in Québec.

LULING CREATURE A creature reported in June, 2005, near San Antonio (Texas). A video recording was made of it. It was hairless, 3' tall and hunchbacked. [120]

LYNX-LIKE CREATURE Creatures so described, not definite lynxes, have been reported from Britain. The *Daily Mirror* described one which was black, seen at Weymouth in 1988. Earlier, one had been seen outside a Devon pub. [#9]

MACAS CREATURE A mammal, about 15"/35cm long, of uncertain species, of which a stuffed specimen was discovered in Macas (Morone-Santiago), Ecuador, in 1999. Although it bears some resemblance to a yapok (*Chironectes minimus*), there are also differences. [#9]

MAFRAQ PREDATOR A mystery animal of Jordan, whose activities took place in 1999. It looked like a cat with a small head, but with large eyes, teeth and tail. Perhaps it was some form of mustelid. Its victims seem to have been pigeons. [N]

MAINE MYSTERY CREATURE A strange creature that has been reported from Maine for a number of years. It is said to be tan and grey with weird eyes and to bear a resemblance to an hyena.   It was blamed for an attack on a Doberman-Pinscher in 2004. [12]

MALABAR A kind of flying snake which the writer Bochart (17th Century) claims is to be found in the Pyrenees. If you lie down when it attacks, it will consider itself the victor and fly away.

MALAYAN APE-MEN In the 1950s there were reports of a trio of hairy "ape-men" – two male, one female – in Malaya (now part of Malaysia). They were said to be hairy and to have fangs. However, they also carried knives and spoke a language, so it seems fairly clear they were humans. The eventual explanation furnished was that they were Nepalis. [#9]

MAN-EATING TREE A tree which supposedly existed on Madagascar. Though mentioned in a number of sources, in origin the story of its existence was a hoax. [L1/A]

MANG A kind of dragon in Chinese legend. [171]

MANGURUYU A sort of monster reported from the Gran Chaco Swamp and Rio Paraguay.

MANN HILL CARCASS A 20' long creature washed up on Mann Hill Beach (Mass.) in 1970. It weighed two tons. It was variously compared with a plesiosaur and a camel. [120]

MAN-SNAKE A snake, large as a coconut tree, which was once a man, in the folklore of Fiji. [G10]

MANTYO Name given to members of a species of giant in which Filipinos believe. They are often to be found near kapok trees. They sleep standing up.

MANX BEAST A creature which looked like a giant chow with no skin on it seen jumping into the sea off the west coast of the Isle of Man in 1910. The creature was reptilian. The witness was the captain of HMS *Caesar*. [146]

MAQUIZCOATL A two-headed snake of Mexican lore. It had red stripes on one side, yellow on the other and black ones on its back. We are told J. Hawkins killed one in 1565. [H17]

MARIANA TRENCH MONSTER Japanese scientists claim to have seen a creature of 180'/60m length in this part of the Pacific in 2003. [34]

MARSHFIELD SEA MONSTER A monster with a crocodilian head and two fins near its tail, with a rounded body, seen off the coast by the ship *Carol Ann* in 1962. [N]

MARTIAN CREATURES The possibility of animals on Mars has been inferred from methane signatures and other evidence by NASA scientists C. Stoker and L. Lemte.

MARUKAR Native American term for a BHM.

MARYLAND MOTHMAN This was seen at 3 a.m. by a Mrs Ruth Lundy, a motorist, in Carroll County. She said it stood like a human, had wings, was coloured brownish-black, had a human-like face, but its chin seemed birdlike. It was over 6' tall. It took off, flying over her car. This is not the only report of a mothman-like creature in Maryland. [162]

MAY RIVER CROCODILIAN The May River system is situated in the Northern Territory of Australia. Here, this creature is supposed to be found. It has many teeth, limbs resembling paddles and is thought to live totally in the water. R. Wells, herpetologist, has been collecting data on this species. [#9]

MAYANJA BEAST A mystery animal said to combine features of lion, leopard and dog reported from this district in Kenya in 1974. It had an appetite for livestock [N]

MBOMBA *see* **SANGU.**

MBULU A reptoid which lives in water, according to Zulu folklore. It has a long tail and its teeth have a sharpish look about them. It seems to be nocturnal, with a propensity to pursue the wayfarer. [A4]

MBULU-EM'BEMBE Ivan Sanderson, noted cryptozoologist, chanced upon tracks of an hippopotamine character in a region of Africa where no hippopotamus dwelt. He was told they had been made by mbulu-eM'bembe, which sounds like another name for mokele-mbembe.. [C/H]

MCCLINTOCK MYSTERY BEAST The tracks of this beast, which was never identified, were found and followed near McClintock Lake (Yukon) in 1913. The tracks indicated the animal was of monstrous proportions and was said to have left a brimstone-like smell around trees on the trail, where it had evidently been tearing at the bark. [N]

MEGA-SHARK A huge creature seen off Port Stephens (New South Wales) in 1918. Estimated lengths varied from 115'-300'. [85]

MEITLIKH Amongst the Indians of the American northwest, a lightning serpent. [186]

MELATHA In Choctaw legend, a male lightning bird. [186]

MELBOURNE CENTAUR A creature that looked like a classical centaur seen by children at Melbourne (Florida) . [154]

MELLING MONSTER A dwarfish creature with avian characteristics reported from Merseyside. [A4]

MENBU LAKE MONSTER The body of this Tibetan monster is said to be very large and its head, set atop a long neck, is quite large as well. It is supposed to have drowned and perhaps eaten a farmer. [22]

MENTIGI MONSTER This was first seen swimming off the Sumatran coast in 2000. Then its carcass was washed up on the shore. It was 18' long, weighed three tons and was said to have tusks. However, sometimes a dead whale can appear to have such appendages.. [120]

MERANAS A French engraving records this fierce mystery animal, at home in the water and on land. One of these animals was put on exhibition at Saint-Pierre (Calvados) and attacked a man who struck it. [155]

MERBOY A young merman. One was reported in Lake Superior in 1782. [H17]

MERMAID *Add to Dictionary article:* A mermaid with long blonde hair was reported off Victoria (British Columbia) in 1967. A number of mermaid sightings are detailed on the message board on the *Fortean Times* website. In the Karoo region of South Africa (once an inland sea) Bushman rock art seems to depict mermaids and some are said to be still reported from Meriningspoort. In case any politically correct individual objects to the word Bushman, it has now become PC to refer to these people as the San. This is because some genius thought that this was their own name for themselves. It isn't. The San are a different people. The Bushmen call themselves the Ju.

MESOPLODON sp. A mystery whale which has been seen, but not classified by science. [C/H]

MEXICAN SABRETOOTH A creature resembling a sabretooth cat was reportedly seen in Mexico in 1994. [#9]

MICHIGAN MONSTER Hirsute monster apparently sojourning on Michigan's Upper Peninsula in the 1960s. [183]

MID-ATLANTIC MONSTER Creature sighted from an American coastguard ship in the 1990s. Its length was estimated at 50' and it circled the ship. It did not blow, as a whale would. It was not recorded in the ship's official report. [C/H]

MILAMO A huge unknown crane reported from Texas. [179]

MILES CANYON DRAGON A beast which, according to Indians of the Yukon, had been killed hundreds of years ago. [N]

MINI-HORSE Two tiny horses 16-18" high were allegedly seen in the Philippines in the 1970s. [1]

MINI-PTERODACTYL Creature reported from Brampton (Ontario), allegedly espied on 1st November, 2004. It had a wingspan of about 4'. [154]

MIRAJ Horned, rabbit-like and fierce creature, apparently supposed to live on some islands in the Indian Ocean. [120]

MIRROR LAKE CREATURE It has the body of a man and the face of a beast, locals will tell you, and it lives in this Alaskan lake. It may originally have been a bogeyman used to keep children from the water margin. [N]

MISSISSIPPI MONSTER A 65' long snakelike beast with a fish tail, a mane and a long beak-like mouth which approached a boat on the Mississippi in 1878. [N]

MISSISSIPPI SHARK A kind of freshwater shark has been reported from the Mississippi. [C1]

M'KE-N'BE A dinosaur-like creature reported from Benin. As its name and description are similar to those of the mokele-mbembe, we are perhaps dealing with the same animal. [E N]

M'KOO A water-dwelling creature, somewhat like a dinosaur in appearance, reported from Africa. [179]

MLOKOKY SMIJ According to Lithuanian legend, these are dragons that supply milk. [171]

MOCCASIN CREEK SNAKE A large snake, possibly a cryptid, seen in this South Dakota locale in 2001.

MOGOLLON MONSTER A BHM reportedly seen in Arizona on the Mogollon Rim and in the Prescott area. One D.Davis, who saw it in 1945, said the face was comparatively hairless.

MOKO A huge lizard which is the object of belief in Mangaia (Cook Islands). He rules all the other lizards. [171]

MONGOLIAN DEATH WORM *Add to Dictionary article:* A Centre for Fortean Zoology expedition in 2005 obtained consistent accounts of the creature from dozens of eyewitnesses. These describe it as scale coloured, 2' long and shaped like a salami. [1]

MONGOLIAN DRAGON The CFZ expedition to Mongolia in 2005 collected reports of a kind of dragon in that country. A living specimen in a well was reported in 2004 near Bulgan, while a dead dragon 100' in length is supposed to have been discovered in the 1940s. [1]

MONGOLIAN HORNED SNAKE Unknown creature said to be over 2m long. [1]

MONKEY MEN Creatures so described were reported by persons taking part in the Texas Water Safari in June, 2005. [120]

MONO CARETO In Spanish folklore, you would see these ugly simians in the Sierra Nevada. [183]

MONSTER FISH This is supposed to occupy Boiling Water Lake (British Columbia).

MONSTER OF GLAMIS *Add to Dictionary article:* There is a suggestion that the monster was a member of the Bowes-Lyon family named Thomas, heir to the earldom of Strathmore, who was born and supposedly died in 1821 and for whom no gravestone can be discovered. In the 1960s it was being said he had been confined in a room off the chapel. [152]

MONTGOMERY MOTHMAN Winged creature that looked like a gargoyle and indulged in a fight with dogs near Montgomery (Alabama). [174]

MOON-EYES A light-sensitive race of tall humans supposed to live beneath the Ozarks.

MOON-MEN I use this term rather than that of *selenites* (employed by H.G. Wells in *The First Men in the Moon*), as it will be more intelligible to readers unfamiliar with Greek. A Latin equivalent might be *lunatics.* According to conspiracy theories, these large humans were seen on the moon by visiting astronauts, who were then compelled to keep quiet about them by unspecified authorities.

Anaxagoras, who was gadding about Greece in ancient times, supposedly said there were houses on the moon, houses implying builders; while both Leonardo da Vinci and Herschel were sure there were moon men. Nor must one forget, in this context, von Gruithuizen (1774-1852), who claimed to have observed a lunar city. However, the belief in their existence runs contrary to the opinions of modern astronomers.

MORCEGO A kind of hominid in Brazilian lore which dwells in burrows or tunnels. [N]

MORRISTOWN MONSTER A strange, apparently bipedal, creature which seemed to lack a head, to be large in size and clumsy of movement (well, wouldn't you be if you hadn't a head?), reported from New Jersey. As I have remarked elsewhere, "headless" creatures may appear so because they hold their heads low in front of their bodies.[A4]

MUD LAKE MONSTER A strange creature seen in Mud Lake (Arkansas) in 1897. It made a whistling noise and was eventually harpooned and dragged ashore by a boatload of locals. These reported it was the weight of an ox, but none could identify it. [G2]

MU-JIMI Alternative name for the hibagon (see *Dictionary*).

MUMELSEE MONSTER Kircher reported a monster in this German lake.

MUMUGA Very strong hairy humanoid in Australian aboriginal legend. [G11]

MURIWAI GLOBSTER Unidentified animal carcass, found in New Zealand in 1965. It seemed to consist of flesh covered by fat covered by skin covered by woolly hair. [120]

MUSCA MACCEDA Giant dangerous fly in the folklore of Sardinia. [J1]

MYSTERY BALEEN WHALE A baleen whale, apparently different from others, which has been noted in the North Atlantic from 1992. Its song has been registered at 52 hertz, a much higher frequency than that of other baleen whales. It may belong to an entirely new species. [#9]

MYSTERY LARVAE Huge numbers of hairy brown larvae of unknown species have been noted in Changdu (Sichuan), China, in 2005. [120]

MYSTERY MANTA RAY Manta rays with white colouration on part of them have been reported from widely separated parts of the world. They may belong to different species. [C/H]

MYSTERY TORTOISE A tortoise, perhaps an unknown species, witnessed by P. Loh in Singapore. He described it as being of medium size. [2]

MYVATN LAKE MONSTER There seems to be a number of such beasts in this Icelandic lake, with long necks and small heads. [N]

NAISH'S GIANT LIZARD In 1997 this was observed crossing a road by well-known cryptozoologist Darren Naish. It was 2 a.m. in the morning and he was helping to push a damaged car when he beheld the creature, 1.5m long or thereabouts, dark in colour with quite a long, heavy neck while the tail was bulky and needed to be dragged along. [#1]

NAKH The nakh, the Estonians assure us, was once a human who drowned. The male now has the shape of a horse or human, the female of a mermaid. They are dangerous to humans, forcing them to dance until they expire.

NALUSA CHITO In Choctaw lore, a creature that carries off women and children, perhaps to eat. Do not confuse with the similarly named *nalusa falaya,* to be found in *Dictionary.* [M11]

NAMIBIAN APE Creature reported from Namibia a number of times in 1959.

NAMIBIAN MYSTERY ANIMAL An animal killed in February, 2005. No one could identify it. It had been hanging around Onava Ya Kiliana village and was thought to have killed animals in the vicinity. [1]

NARSINGA According to Bochart (16th Century), a kind of flying snake to be found in the Pyrenees. These are poisonous and their poison is very painful.

NAV A large bird in which Serbs, Croats and Bulgarians believe. The Serbs and Croats say navs have children's heads. [155]

NEW BRITAIN DINOSAUR On the island of New Britain, Papua-New Guinea, this creature, 3m tall with a canine head and crocodilian tail, was observed. The animal is supposed to have eaten three dogs. [12]

NEW JERSEY VEGETABLE MONSTER A creature looking like a stick of broccoli, reported by an inebriate. The term has been extended to cover any cryptid for which there is very poor evidence.

NEW RIVER INLET MONSTER In 1885 a creature looking like a plesiosaur was dragged up by a ship's anchor at this Florida locale. [166]

NEW ZEALAND WEIRD ANIMAL A slim, furry, long-tailed, speedy, pig-sized animal observed in New Zealand. The observer failed to identify it. [85]

NEWPORT CREATURE Seen at Newport (Tennessee) in 2004, this creature resembled an arrowhead flying in the wrong direction. In fact it seemed to glide rather than fly and its appendages for doing this resembled those of a flying squirrel. Its height was judged at 3', its width at the shoulder 2'. [1]

NEZ PERCÉ MONSTER Primeval monster in Nez Percé lore which swallowed the whole human race, but which was killed by Coyote. [169]

NGANI-VATU A huge bird of Fijian belief, not reported since the 19th Century. [N]

NGEND Kind of ape in the legends of Cameroon. Its left arm is said not to function, while its right arm contains a spike. It usually, but not invariably, keeps to the trees.

NGOUBOU A West African cryptid. It is said to be the size of an ox, to have two horns above the eyes and a small one on the nose and a bony frill. It can kill elephants. [180]

NGUAT-NGUAT A kind of hairy humanoid found in the western part of Victoria, according to Australian aboriginal tradition. It was said to be of human height and to suck blood. [G11]

NGWEMPISI RIVER MONSTER This beastie was observed in South Africa in 1950. [E]

NHANG This creature, a mixture of crocodile and seal, springs from Armenian legend. It is supposed to be found in the rivers Euphrates and Murat Nehri. [C/H]

NIGHT APE Term for a BHM used in Sulphur River (Texas). [183]

NINGBO CITY MONSTER Monster found stranded, dead and decomposing, on a wall at this city in China's Zheijing province in July, 2005. It is nearly 12m long and unidentifiable. [2]

NINKO FOX A variety of the werefox or kitsune in Japanese lore. It is actually a spiritual being. It can possess people. [H16]

NOGITSUNE In Japanese lore, a werefox that is mischievous or evil.

NORTH AMERICAN UNICORN Elizabethan mariner John Hawkins saw one in Florida. He described it as gleaming white. Unicorns were also reported in the vicinity of the Canadian border in the 17th Century. There were also supposed to be unicorns in New York state. These had shaggy manes, a stag's neck and a wild pig's tail. [H17]

NORTON MERE MONSTER A possible monster was inferred from a wake in this Shropshire lake in 1973 [#9]

NORWICH FOX A mysterious fox seen near Norwich in 1994. White, with comparatively short legs, it may have been an Arctic fox.

NUE Legendary evil-bearing creature of Japanese folklore, with the head of a monkey, the body of a racoon-like dog, a tiger's legs and a snake instead of a tail. [152]

NUNDA An alternative form of **Nundu.**

OBONI Primate with a human-like face observed in Thailand in 1970. [183]

OCTOPOD Term applied to a cryptobotanical tree of Brazil. [179]

ODENTON CREATURE In the 1960s two nocturnal drivers encountered a strange beast in Maryland. It was 10' tall, had protuberant eyeballs and green slimy hair. One has the impression that it was bipedal, but this is not explicitly stated. P. Rife regards it as a lizard man, but the hair would tend to belie this. [R6]

OHIO CREATURE A creature seen by a motorist which he was inclined to compare with a mothman, but he discerned no wings. It was bipedal, of human size and white/grey in colour. [174]

OHIO PTERODACTYL This creature, resembling a pterodactyl, with 15-29' wings, was seen by James Morgan, near Middletown, Ohio, in 1967. [154]

OLAK Alaskan name for a BHM. [1]

ON NIONT A water creature of Huron legend, it looks like a horned snake.

ONCA-CANGUCU An animal that looks like a large black felid with a white collar about its throat. [#9]

ONE-EYED MONSTER A strange and large monster, seen off the American coast. A Captain Neil, describing it in 1834, said the part of its head above the water measured about 12'. One assumes this includes the neck. Captain Neil was not the only one to describe it. [H17]

ONE-HORNED CATTLE These were reported in Somalia by the traveller Lodovico de Varthema in the 16th Century. They were perhaps beasts whose horns had been artificially joined.

ORANG MINYAK Legendary primate of Malaysia. The orang minyak is said to be smaller than the orang dalam.

OREGON CREATURE Observed on 4th July, 195, it was a strange creature seen at night in a river in Oregon. Its head, adorned with wisps of hair, was shaped like a bullet. Its body had short brown hair all over it. It had huge eyes that covered about half its head. Its shape was humanoid. [154]

OROCHI An eight-headed dragon in Japanese mythology slain by the god Susanoo. The latter drugged him, then cut off his eight heads. This, I feel, is a very sensible way to deal with eight-headed dragons.

PABLO CREATURE Unidentified grey animal killed by a dog in Pablo (Montana) in 1980. It was quite small in size.

PADUCAH CREATURE A white animal about the size of a German shepherd/Alsatian that largely resembled a sloth. Its fur was shaggy. The sighting took place at Paducah (Kentucky).   [2]

PAHAZO Paiute Indian name for a BHM. [183]

PAJAR A bird of Romanian legend, based ultimately upon the pelican.

PALENQUE CREATURE The Mayan carvings at Palenque (Mexico) depict a mystery creature with clawed hands and feet attacking men. [180]

PALMQVIST CREATURE A small animal found in a packet of shrimp by Karin and Kenneth Palmqvist. It looked like a tiny crocodile – it could fit in one hand – and had a pair of fins which could have been nascent legs. It also boasted a pair of antennae. Attempts to identify it with the fish *Chimera monstrosa* are not altogether convincing. [34]

PANKALANKA In the Northern Territory of Australia, this term is used to mean a sort of apelike animal.

PARBROATH CAT A grey mystery cat with black markings seen in Scotland in 2002. It was very hairy. [167]

PELADIT In the Montserrat Mountains of Spain it is said you will encounter this creature which exhibits features of human and bear and is also said to be a marsupial. [183]

PENG A monstrous fish of Chinese lore that could transform into a bird. [152]

PENNSYLVANIA TOAD A large toad, dark in colour, which covered the metal part of a miner's coal shovel. Witness Melissa Barclay claimed that it was about 14" in length and 1' in width. Its skin was rougher than that of normal toads in the area. Her father dug it out from under 2' of earth and it at length hopped away. This occurred in 1973 at Forward township (Pa.). [2]

PEORIA PREDATOR A mystery animal reported from Illinois which gave tongue to lusty roars and killed many a pig and chicken in 1950. [N]

PETERSFIELD MONKEY Hairless creature that generally resembled a monkey seen by a school student in Petersfield, England. It boasted fangs 2-2.5" long. [2]

PHENG Gigantic bird of Japanese legend, it could swallow a camel, which, I believe, is no easy task. [B19]

PICHU-CUATE A tiny snake, about the size of a lead pencil, encountered by C.F. Lummis in the 19th Century. Local Indians spoke in awe of its ferocity and venom. The creature may now be extinct. There is evidence that the term *pichu-cuate* has been applied to other snakes. [A5]

PIG-FISH A strange fish captured in the Danube in 1997. Its body was piglike, the head and tail being completely piscine. Bony plates covered its body. [155]

PINCHULAO BEAST A creature 1' in length killed in Chile when surprised drinking chicken's blood. Some thought it might be the chupacabras, but could not be certain. [N]

PINK FOX Small peach-pink animal seen by a child in Quebec in 1996. [2]

PIVA LIZARD A giant reptile about 10m long with a snakelike head and legs like a green lizard's, which was seen entering and crossing the River Piva in Bosnia in the 1980s. Reports of similar creatures from elsewhere in Bosnia and from Montenegro are not unknown. [155]

PIXIU Creature of Chinese lore looking like a lion with a dragon's head. It is the ninth child of a dragon. The male is called *pi*, the female *xiu*. [152]

PLANO CREATURE This was seen at Plano (Texas) in 1979. It moved by hopping in slow motion, was estimated at 10' tall and had pointed ears. [187]

PLANTE VAMPIRE Cryptobotanical plant of Mexico. It eats birds. [179]

PLAVKO Name given to an alleged monster in Lake Plavska in Montenegro. Its presence has been inferred from strange sounds, which scientists ascribe to underground streams. [155]

POISON BLENNY A variety of blenny said to be found in the waters of Iran. [174]

POMORNIK A beast compared with the chupacabras which has been reported from Pomorze Zachodnie in Poland. It is said to have killed more than 200 animals. [2]

PONTARF It was believed in the Middle Ages that this was a child-snatching fish of Europe.

PONTEFRACT SNAKE According to legend, a giant snake was once to be found near Pontefract in Yorkshire. It was killed in a battle with a shepherd and his dog, to whom the battle also proved fatal. [C1]

POPE LICK MONSTER Beneath the Pope Lick trestle at Louisville (Kentucky) lurks the Pope Lick Monster. It will scare you off by screaming or hurling stones at you. Some say it looks like a human with a goat's head, some that it looks like a white yeti. [182]

PORTAFERRIO OCTOPUS An unusual nine-tentacled octopus (if that isn't a contradiction in terms) with what looked like a porcupine's spines was reported captured off the Italian coast in 1914. [155]

PORTO RECANTI CREATURE A creature described so strangely that its nature is very obscure, observed off the Italian coast in 1894. Called a 'female dolphin', it is said to have looked like a human without arms or legs. [155]

PROCTOR VALLEY MONSTER The story of this creature is that of a well-known urban legend. A car with a young couple in it stalls. The male emerges. The female hears scratching on the roof. It turns out to have been the monster placing the male's body there. This tale has been localised in Proctor Valley (California). The local museum has what passes for a cast of the monster's footprint. The story is certainly as old as the 1960s. It has been made the subject of a musical. [12]

PUERTO RICO CREATURE A short creature resembling an ape, hairy and dark brown, which was seen on a roof by a boy and his grandmother about 1962. The creature had wings and flew off. [154]

PYRAMID LAKE MONSTER A kind of demon, whose footprints may be discerned on the lake bottom, in the beliefs of the Indians near Pyramid Lake (Nevada). [E]

PYRENEAN SERPENT According to Topsell, this is a flying serpent that does not exceed 4' in length and is as thick as a man's arm.

QUEEN CHARLOTTE ISLANDS MONSTER Serpentine creature 25' long with a fishtail reported by two witnesses off the Queen Charlotte Islands in 1897. [1]

QUINOTAUR Certain Frankish rulers claimed descent from "a beast like a quinotaur". Presumably, a quinotaur has something of the bull about it. Maybe it was originally a misreading of minotaur.

RADISSON'S REPTILE It looked like a large black snake with a very big head and four legs and was encountered in what is now New York state by P. Raddison and the Sieur de Groseilliers. [H17]

RAILALOMENA This unknown creature is said to dwell in the waters of Madagascar and to boast a single horn. [179]

RANDOLPH COUNTY ANIMAL A fox-sized animal with a tail like a cat's and short brown hair, first seen near Asheboro (North Carolina) about Christmas, 2004. [1]

RASA MONSTER Creature seen and photographed in the Rasa River, Croatia, in 2002.

RAT-SHARK Rat-sharks are horrible water-dwelling creatures in the folklore of Kauai (Hawaii). Although they look like large rats, each has a shark's mouth on its back, with which it can devour the hapless swimmer. [G10]

RATTLESNAKE HILL DRAGON Rattlesnake Hill lies near Silver Run (Maryland) and here a fiery dragon was reported in 1783. [N]

RAVINE BEAST Dylan Hallowbrass claimed to have seen an animal 7' in height with a porcine head, long neck, thick fur and generally massive appearance attack a deer in a ravine in an unspecified location some time in 2004. He and his two friends then saw two more of the creatures. [154]

RED HEADBAND A giant wearing a red headband said to live in or near the crater of Mount Karthala (Comoros). A number of people have claimed sightings. [12]

RED RAVEN Red ravens of gigantic size were reported in the Roman sky in 106 BC. [1]

RED-FURRED CREATURE Bipedal creature about the size of an emu, with red fur. It had antlers and, although its body resembled that of a bird, it lacked wings and feathers. It was seen by two boys about 1999 at Lampasas (Texas). [154]

REPTOID A reptilian being, which conspiracy theorists argue exists or existed. A race of reptoids is postulated. Thus David Icke (born 1952) maintains the world is ruled by reptoids who seem to be doing this from what he calls the lower fourth dimension. No, I don't know where that is supposed to be either. Reptoids figure in other conspiracy literature as well. A man claiming he had been a security guard at Dulce Air Force Base (New Mexico) maintained they were to be found there too. The actual existence of this base, however, is not certainly established: it exists in conspiracy theories and is supposedly underground. The Terrestrial Reptoid Hypothesis, which maintains that reptoids live in cities under the earth, has been advocated by J. Rhode. Some persons believe in a kind of élite reptilian race called the Draco-Reptilians which are credited with wings and blunt horns. They are sometimes said to wear capes. Modern conspiracy theorists have even suggested Hitler escaped to the Antarctic, where he is being cared for by solicitous reptoids.

REXBEAST Huge hominid, larger than a yowie, which cryptozoologist Rex Gilroy avers still exists, as he has discovered its tracks. [N]

RIDGE ROAD CREATURE A large creature that looked like a primate. It was seen twice by members of the same family on a road in Blair County (Pa). The father, who saw it first, said it was taller than a man, apparently hairless and of a grey colour which was described as "ghastly". Years later, the son had a similar sighting. [A5]

ROANE A creature of Scottish folklore which seems much the same as a selkie; cf. Gaelic *ron*, 'seal'.

ROCK SLIDE BOLTER A huge creature of the salamander or lizard variety believed by many to exist in the Black Forest (Colorado). Some, however, have dismissed the story as a tall tale. [2]

ROCK SWALLOW Fierce birds of Navaho myth were so called. [R8]

ROMAN DRAGON This creature is supposed to have lived in a cave near Rome in 1651. [165]

ROTSEE DRAGON A creature which emerged from this Swiss lake in 1599 for a spot of sunbathing. There may have been earlier sightings. [N]

ROUGE RIVER MONSTER It looks like a monster, it has purple ears and a blue tail and it is allegedly found in this river near Toronto. It is 14" long and locals call it Lenny the Lizard. [N]

RUNAN SHAH *see* **Caspian Fish man.**

RUNNING ROCK There were two of these living rocks in Jicarillo Apache legend.

They were killed by Killer of Enemies. [L5]

RUREN A kind of manlike creature mentioned by the Chinese author Liu Yiqing (5th Century AD).

RYUKYU KINGFISHER A supposedly extinct bird (*Halcyon myakoensis*). Some reports indicate that it may still survive.

SABRE-TOOTHED CAT P. Matthiesen in his book *The Cloud Forest* (1966) tells of hearing of such a creature in South America, smaller than a jaguar and of a somewhat timid disposition.

SAMEBITO A kind of merman with the tail of a shark in Japanese lore. [P2]

SANGU The Wele of central Africa worship this large water monster which is also known as Mbomba. [K5]

SARKANY A polycephalous dragon in Hungarian legend. [186]

SARRASIN Sarrasins were wildmen of Alpine folklore, who were in the habit of begging food from humans. One was reported as recently as 1954 in Isere. [183]

SCALY HORSE A horselike creature with scales, spotted in the sea off the Orkney Islands in 1902. [146]

SCYLLA A monster of Greek mythology, a mixture of woman, dog and fish.

SEA DRAGON *Add to Dictionary article:* **3** A fire-breathing dragon observed from Christchurch (Dorset) around the year 1113. [146]

SEA HUMAN Sea creatures that bore some similarities to humans were said to have been washed up in the Azores in 1876. [1]

SEA MAN A kind of sea-dwelling creature shot by a sentry at Boulogne-sur-Mer, France, about 1764. [155]

SEA MONKEY Creature half monkey half fish illustrated in the *Hortus sanitatis* (1491).

SEA PLATYPUS A creature 6' long which bore some resemblance to the Australian duck-billed platypus or ornithorhynchus has been reported in the seas off the Alaskan coast. [#11]

SEA SERPENT *Add to Dictionary article:* A possible sea serpent was seen off the Norwegian coast in August, 2004, by swimmers, but the possibility that it was a boa-constrictor has also been mentioned.

SEA TURK A curious creature illustrated in the *Hortus sanitatis* (1491). The lower half was fishlike, the upper looked like an oriental, including a turban, which was presumably regarded as part of the creature rather than a garment.

SEA WOLF Alternative name for the Sproat Lake Monster.

SEALPSEE DRAGON There is supposed to be a dragon in the Sealpsee, a Bavarian lake. [N]

SELMA MOTHMAN A humanoid with wings observed for about half an hour in Selma (Alabama) in 1948. [154]

SERBIAN FLYING SNAKE This creature allegedly bit a boy named Dusan Pjevaca, who threw it into a furnace. Its bite did not prove poisonous. [155]

SHADHAHVAR A single-horned antelope of Persian lore. Music played by the wind blowing into its horn attracts its victims.

SHAN GUI Chinese and Vietnamese hominid. It has been referred to for hundreds of years. [N]

SHAPINSAY BEAST It looked like a horse, seemed to be spotted and scaly and was seen in 1902 off the Orkney coast. [146]

SHEDU Winged bull of Akkadian mythology.

SHEFFIELD WODEWOSE A kind of wildman reported from Graves Park, a 200-acre region near Sheffield. It seems to have been a kind of otherworldly entity. It was once seen as a green mist, once as something somewhat more solid. [85]

SHETI A race of subterranean reptoids in Hopi Indian belief.

SHETLAND CREATURE A mystery creature observed in the sea near the Shetland Islands on a number of occasions. It looks like a sail and has a flipper on the end of its nose. [146]

SIDNEY HUMANOID This creature leaped from 50-60'. It had a grey face, while its eyes glowed red. It was seen in 1973 in Sidney (North Carolina). [85]

SIMIOT A sort of black hairy humanoid once said to have been found in the Pyrenees. [183]

SINILIND Blue bird in Estonian mythology.

SIOUX CITY MOTHMAN A large creature with wings and two red eyes reported by a duo named Lance and Nick. [174]

SITUATE HARBOR MONSTER A 50' carcass which was washed up in Situate Harbor (Mass.). Witnesses declared it was a sea-monster, but it was badly damaged by onlookers before it could be examined. [165]

SKADEGAMUTC The Micmac Indians say this creature will follow you and hide from you behind trees. It is noted for its shrieks. There doesn't seem to be evidence of its appearance. [A4]

SKANEATELES LAKE FISH A strange-looking fish with an unusual head, perhaps an unknown form of sturgeon, was sighted in July, 2005, in New York state. [120]

SKANICUM A cave-dwelling BHM in the legendry of the Lake Band Indians. [178]

SKEGNESS CREATURE This snakelike beast has been reported off the Lancashire coast since the 1930s. [146]

SMALL-HEADED FLYCATCHER This bird was reported in New Jersey in the early 19th Century and has now done a disappearing act. Some say it never existed at all and was the result of mistaken observations; some that it was indeed seen, but is now extinct.

SMOK WAWELSKI A Polish dragon who met his end either at the hands of Prince Krakus (who founded Krakow over his remains) or a cobbler's apprentice named Szewczyk Dratewka. [182]

SNAKE WITH LEGS This creature was black and white with yellow spots and seems to have been a lizard rather than a snake. It was seen in 19th Century Ohio. A child was saved from its clutches. [N]

SNOMANNEN A kind of Wildman, said to be found in the forests, in Swedish belief. Another name for this creature would seem to be *Kinderfresser*, devourer of children. *See also* **Swedish Wildman** in *Dictionary*. [#9]

SOUTH DAKOTA DINOSAUR A dinosaur-like creature attacked a farmer in 1934, forcing his tractor off the road, near Lake Campbell (South Dakota). [R6]

SPECKLED TIGER Peruvian cryptid, grey in colour with speckles, with a jaguar-sized body and a head larger than a jaguar's. [153]

SPOOK HOLLOW CREATURE A creature seen in Maryland. It had hairless skin, but a human-like face. It was reckoned to be about the size of a yearling bear. The witnesses identified it as a ghost, but there seems to have been no warrant for this. [A5]

STENWYKEN A kind of BHM supposed to inhabit the Okanagan Valley (British Columbia), according to Indian legend. [178]

ST-PLAH In the lore of the Indians of the Pacific Northwest of the USA, a race of water dwelling giants. Of solitary bent, they lived at the bottoms of ponds and lakes. They would seize the startled passer-by and make of him a meal or a menial. [170]

STRANGE CRITTER This was the name given by One-Eye Bascomb to an animal he saw in Oklahoma in 1849. It seems to have been a hominid or wildman.

STRANGE RODENT A pair of rodents with the naked tails of rats, but the rounded faces of hamsters were spotted in the San Joaquin Valley (Ca.) in June, 2005. As yet their identity is a mystery. [2]

STRIPED BIG CAT A creature known in Cherokee tradition. The actual Cherokee word which is here rendered 'big cat' could not be translated by the person who was told of it, but it does seem to have been both large and feline. [2]

STRIPED FOX Such a creature has been reported from Croydon (Surrey). [85]

STRIPED TIGER Peruvian cryptid, about the size of a jaguar, but with stripes like a tiger. [153]

SUBTERRANEAN MUTANTS These are to be found in the tunnels under London, modern folklore suggests. They are supposedly descended from humans who went to live below ground in the 19th Century.

SUFFOLK SEA MONSTER The *Gentleman's Magazine* for 1750 reports the capture of this beast. It was 5' in length, its head resembled a dog's, it had a beard (?mane) like a lion's, it was covered with down and had spots. It was of a gentle disposition.

SUMATRAN HUMMINGBIRD There aren't supposed to be any hummingbirds outside the Americas, but sightings of one were allegedly made in 1957 and 1958. These may, however, have been due to misidentifications. [N]

SUSSEX COUNTY PREDATOR Mystery predator reported from Sussex County (New Jersey) in 2005. It had killed a miniature horse. Various theories regarding its identity, including the cryptozoological, were mooted. [1]

SUWARROW ISLAND DEVILFISH Monstrous carcass with a pair of tusks and a covering of hair stranded in Samoa in the 19th century. It was 60' long and the skull was 3'. It was estimated to weigh 70 tons. [120]

TAGUA TAGUA MONSTER Search for the Tagua Tagua lagoon in Chile and you won't find it - it was drained some time ago. However, in 1784 a monster allegedly quitted the lagoon and caused some havoc on the farm of Don Próspero Elso. It was supposedly caught. An etching was made of the beast. It had wings, two tails and a face. [154]

TAHITI SEA SERPENT This creature, said to dwell off the isle of Tahiti, used to demand a human sacrifice per annum. [G10]

TAPIR-IAUARA A cryptid reported from a large area of South America. It has red or red-golden fur, its face looks like a jaguar's, it has bovine floppy ears and legs like a donkey's. Whether it has hooves remains uncertain, as it tends to favour a watery habitat. Its coat is both glowing and waterproof. [168]

TARROO-USHTEY The water-bull of Manx legend. It closely resembles domestic cattle. [A.W. Moore *Folklore of the Isle of Man*, 1891].

TASMANIAN MYSTERY CREATURE An animal observed by a night-time driver. It looked like a cat with a monkey's face. [2]

TEINIAGUÁ In Brazilian legend, a magic lizard which guards a treasure. [185]

TEMU A small unknown primate reported from Liberia. [H7]

TENNESSEE CREATURE This was seen by a small child in Rutherford County. The creature was sitting on a neighbour's doorstep. It was man-sized with a camel-like head and a covering of what was possibly white fur. It had a fat stomach. [85]

THERENDE A killing animal on the rampage near Caen in 1632-3. It appears to have been canine. [155]

THYLACINE *Add to Dictionary article:* A magazine called the *Bulletin* has offered a reward of A$1.25 million for a legally captured specimen of the animal, while Thylacine Expeditions has offered a reward to A$1.75 million. *See also* **British thylacine.**

TIGER-DOG An unidentified animal, perhaps a coati, captured in Long Branch (Indiana) in 1903. [N]

TIREE BEAST A 50'/15m beast which looked like a lizard with a long neck attacked a vessel off Tiree (Scotland) in 1934. [146]

TIZZIE-WIZZIE A strange creature reported from the vicinity of Lake Windemere (Cumbria) and said to have features resembling both a hedgehog and a squirrel. It is also said to have wings like a bumble-bee. A boatman claimed to have seen it in 1900 and an apparent specimen was captured and photographed in 1906, though, to the best of my knowledge, no examination was made. Other reports have come in over the years. A couple of sightings were reported in May, 2005.

TONGUE-EATER Mystery predator of Nicaragua, reported in 1997, supposed to combine features of turkey and cat. (Honestly, I don't make these things up). It would remove its victims' tongues, unlike the chupacabras. [N]

TOTONGE A huge monster, an unknown creature, in the legends of the Lokanda of the Congo (Kinshasa). We are told, however, that it has at least one hand. [K5]

TRANSLUCENT TURKEY This huge bird has been reported from Wales. Those who have encountered it say it twirls around, growing larger the whole time. It is so frightening that no one has lingered long enough to find out what happens when it stops twirling. [S1*]

TRAPA TRAPA CREATURE Diminutive being with large head seen in Argentina in 2000. [187]

TREE MAN Tree men, in the lore of the Coeur d'Alene Indians, were in fact were-trees. [177]

TRITON The ancient Greeks believed in creatures that were like men to the waist and like dolphins below. These were the tritons. The females were called tritonids. [P2]

TROJAN A creature of Russian legend, said to live in the mountains. It is nocturnal, has three heads and an ass's ears. [155]

TROPICAL BOTTLENOSE WHALE An as yet unclassified cetacean, a kind of beaked whale. [C/H]

TROUGH OF BOLAND CREATURE A bipedal creature that supposedly exsanguinated a sheep in north-west England. One of the witnesses fired at its retreating form. The second opined that the chupacabras had reached England. [176]

TSE'NENAXA'LI A monster of Navaho myth with a long beak and large eyes. [R8]

TUMBLING RUN MONSTER Beast resembling a snake, 15' in length, sighted near the Tumbling Run Dam in Pennsylvania. [12]

TUNDRA HORSE Siberian variety of horse, possibly extinct, though what may be a surviving group was seen in 1964. They were white in colour.

TURKISH CREATURE A strange animal seen making a nocturnal road crossing in 2003, about 90km from Istanbul. It was hairless, silver-grey, its back was arched and it lacked a tail. It rose to its hind legs and stood about 1.65m tall. [187]

TURKMENISTAN LION The Asiatic lion (*Panthera pardus persica*) had long been thought to be confined to the Gir Forest in India. Now, however, a sighting of a possible specimen in Turkmenistan has shown in may yet linger there. [#1]

TZARS POND CREATURE In 1997 fishermen are supposed to have encountered an octopus-like creature at this locale in Serbia. [155]

UGALLU A benevolent supernatural being in Mesopotamian mythology. Its body was human, but it had the head of a lion and the feet of a bird.

UMDHLEBI A crypto-botanic tree. The Zulus, who believe in it, will not approach it, as it generates poison gas. [179]

UNIPED A one-footed humanoid supposedly found in North America. Jacques Cartier (1491-1557) was told of these creatures. [H17]

UNKNOWN ANT In 1895 it was reported that ants of unknown species and enormous size fell out of the sky in Manitoba. [F7]

UNKNOWN FELID The book *The Master of Game* (15th Century) is now to be found in the Bodleian Library, Oxford. It features an illustration of what is possibly a leopard, but may be also a new species of cat. It might also be a cheetah, as these were used for hunting in medieval France. [#1]

UNKNOWN SWIFT Unknown varieties of swift have been reported from both Africa and China. *See also* **Whiskered Swift** in *Dictionary*. [#9]

UNKTEHI Creature in the lore of the Sioux Indians. It looks like a snake with four legs, a horn on its head and a spiked tail. It is supposed to live in the Missouri. [N]

URISEE MONSTER A creature reported from this Austrian lake in the 19th Century. It should not be confused with the Swiss Urnersee Monster, which was a hoax.

UROO Subterranean water serpent in Australian Aboriginal belief.

UTICA GOATMAN A creature that looked like a human from the waist up, a goat from the waist down. It was observed near Utica (Nebraska) in 1982. [85]

UWIBAMI Celebrated man-eating dragon of Japanese lore. [160]

VALPARAISO CREATURE The corpse of a strange creature was discovered in a kennel in Valparaiso in 2004. It may have been somewhat decomposed and was certainly not easy on the nose. It has been sent for scientific testing, but may prove to be nothing more than a cat or dog. [28]

VANARA Large kind of monkey mentioned in Hindu legend. [12]

VANCOUVER ISLAND SEA SERPENT A creature observed by two witnesses in 1905. There were two bumps on its head, but it was difficult to make out its eyes. [1]

VETULARCTOS A rather mysterious bear killed in Canada in 1864 and now to be found stuffed in the National Museum of that country. While it may belong to an unknown species (*Vetularctus inopinatus*), it is possibly merely an unusual grizzly or a grizzly/polar bear hybrid. [2]

VEULETTE SEA SERPENT A large and speedy serpentine creature seen off the French coast in 1881. [155]

VIBNA Term for a kind of dragoness in Catalan lore. It has female breasts and a large beak.

VILKACIS A monster that had originally been a man in the traditions of the Latvians. Its name means "wolf's eyes". [152]

VILLA SAN RAFAEL CREATURE A creature reported to have been seen at this location in Chile in 2002. Two teenagers saw this creature which looked like a rugby football with legs. A kind of energy like an electric shock in the stomach proceeded from it. It progressed by leaps. [#1]

VIRGINIA MOTHMAN An 8-12' tall humanoid with "wing-like arms" seen near Haymarket (Virginia) by four men in the 1960s. [R6]

WABASH RIVER CREATURE This Indiana river played host to a strange creature with a leonine head reported in the 1890s. [S10]

WALADHEGARRA Small hirsute hominids in Australian aboriginal legend. [G11]

WANJILANKO A stump-tailed, long-fanged (?sabre-toothed), red-coated, striped, lion-killing cat of Senegal. [N]

WASAGA BEACH CREATURE A large mystery beast like a seal was observed at this location in Georgian Bay (Ontario) in 1938. There have been other reports of strange creatures in the bay. [172]

WAST WATER MONSTER Wast Water (Cumbria) is England's deepest lake. It is said to house a monster. [146]

WATERFORD LIZARD This fierce reptile attacked a car containing two teenagers in Waterford, a suburb of Detroit (Michigan), in 1973. There was a lake nearby, but there is nothing to indicate this was the beast's habitat.

WAWANAR Legendary flying creature of New Guinea. [2]

WECHUGE Large, rough-looking humanoid in the lore of the Athabascan Indians. Wechuges are not necessarily gigantic, however. They are hairy and eat people. Uncontrolled emotion can turn an ordinary person into a wechuge. [G10]

WELSH CREATURE A creature reported from near Pont-y-Glyn. It is of horrid aspect, has, it is thought, a single eye, long sharp teeth and long arms of withered aspect which end in talons. It will sail away into the air. [S1*]

WELSH FLYING CREATURE This was seen by a number of witnesses over Llangollen in 1905. Its body was somewhat porcine, its feet webbed. [146]

WELSH KOALA Sightings of Welsh koalas were reported in the 1990s. On what such animals might have subsisted poses a serious question. [146]

WERECROCODILE These are reportedly found in West Africa and sound better avoided.

WEREFOX Apart from the kitsune of Japan, werefoxes are found in the legends of other countries. One such legend features a werefox at Wagon Mound (New Mexico) – it was wounded and later the wound was found on an old woman. In some tales, werefoxes are in fact foxes that turn into humans. The Eskimos and Incas tell of such beings. In China werefoxes are generally, but not invariably, benevolent. They are there called *o-tsze*. [H16]

WEREJAGUAR Folklore creature in Brazil which, in human form, is a woman with more than the usual complement of nipples. In Guiana, they believe in what they call kanaima jaguars, humans who change into jaguar form and which are often thought to have a taste for human flesh. [156 H16]

WEREKANGAROO Should you encounter a large kangaroo that does not retreat on your approach, the Aborigines will tell you it is a werekangaroo. [H16]

WERERABBIT In agricultural folklore rabbits are treated with a certain alarm, as they are thought to be possible witches in disguise. [P3]

WERE-SHARK Such creatures are supposed to exist in waters off Java, Tonga, Hawaii and Fiji. [10]

WEREWOLF *Add to Dictionary article:* Werewolves have not been invariably regarded as evil. The Zuñi werewolf, White Wolf Woman, is regarded as benevolent. The ghost of a werewolf (who was the son of a witch) is supposed to haunt part of Michigan to this day. A sighting was reported in 1986. Another werewolf ghost is supposed to be found in Brandywine Park (Pennsylvania). Werewolf sightings were reported from Texas in 1971. In the same year a female werewolf was allegedly seen in Mobile (Alabama). You might well expect to find werewolves at Mount Loup-Garou in Québec, although an expedition of students thither in 1954 failed to discover any. [H16]

WESK'EKKEHS A creature in the legends of the Penobscot Indians, its name means "great hairless bear". *See also* **Great Naked Bear.**

WEST AFRICAN BEAST A mysterious creature known only by its tracks. The Abbé Proyhart described them in 1776. The footprints were clawed and some were as large as 3' in diameter.

WHITE ANIMAL A number of these creatures were reported from Shoshone (Idaho) in April, 2005. They were humanoid or anthropoid and pure white. They lacked ears and eyes and their mouths were vestigial. They were gorging themselves on fish and placing large quantities of them in kangaroo-like pouches. [181]

WHITE APE This beast was reported in the desert near Santa Fé (New Mexico) in 1966.

WHITE DEMON A humanoid seen in Richland (Washington) in 1966. Although it was shot at, it was either unhit or impervious to bullets. It gave vent to some loud screams, however. [G7]

WHITE FOX Mystery fox, not an albino or Arctic fox, seen in Ohio about 1998. [2]

WHITE THING A white creature reported in Du Quoin (Illinois) in 1967. The witness on first glimpse thought it a dog, then saw it had an eyeless, human-like face with merely holes for ears. It had hands and human-like feet and lacked a tail. Its mouth was a slit. [181]

WHOOSH CAT Near Memphis (Tennessee) witness Jeff Crook felt a compulsion to walk to the corner of his house. He heard a whooshing sound like the wind, but no wind was blowing. Then a grey felid, long-legged and about 3' tall at the shoulder, ran across his drive and went out of sight over a hilltop. [85]

WILDMAN *Add to Dictionary article:* R. Bernheimer argues that the figure of the European wildman was part of a cult. He cites the practice of a wildman hunt (in which the wildman was played by a human) and folk festivals in support of this. He feels that the wildman originally personified winter and was ritually slain. He further advances the possibility that playing the part of the wildman in such celebrations was in fact an initiation into some kind of secret society.

A curious belief obtained in Europe that the wildman enjoyed bad weather and was made miserable by good. He was also, like the fairies, supposed to steal human children and leave changelings in their place, according to Swiss traditions of the Grisons. Depictions of the wildman sometimes show him carrying a roughly hewn cudgel.

The wildman ate food raw and could not make fire. An engraving of a wildman by Israhel van Meckenem (16th Century) shows a creature resembling Billy Connolly with additional hair.

Paracelsus (1493-1541) averred wildmen have human reason, but no souls. He does not seem to regard sexual contact with wild women as uncommon. [B19 B20]

WINDIGO *Add to Dictionary article:* One wonders if the windigo is not in origin a personification of winter, perhaps augmented by sightings of Bigfoot. It certainly seems to be associated with bad weather, destruction of woodlands and depression, often an adjunct of the dark winter months. Some Indians seem to believe that all windigos were once humans who acquired their nature. Sometimes the windigo may encapsulate negative antisocial desires in the human psyche.

WINDSOR BEAST A mystery animal that killed sheep near Windsor and Guildford in 1906.

WINEMBU Diminutive man-beasts in the Aboriginal lore of New South Wales. [G11]

WINGED FISH In Cusick's *History of the Six Nations* (1823), an Iroquois expedition encountered this creature in prehistoric times. It flitted about amongst the trees.

WINTERFOLD CREATURE It was about 140cm tall, had an oblong glowing head and a sharp smell. It was seen on a road in this Surrey location in 1967. [146]

WISCONSIN WILD MAN Whether this was a Bigfoot, a lunatic or something else, it was captured in Chippewa County (Wisconsin) in 1895 and housed in the county jail, where it appears to have resided for ten years. [R4]

WIT VROUW VAN DIE BRANDENBURG A peculiar humanoid figure, white on top, black below, found in a Namibian cave painting. Whether it indicates some strange creature with which the artist was familiar is unknown. [173]

WOCHWOSEN Gigantic bird, enemy of a certain thunderbird, in the legends of the Passamaquaddy Indians. [169]

WODEWOSE *Add to Dictionary article:* A contributor to the *Fortean Times* Message Board said he read somewhere that a wodewose was captured in the early 20th Century, carrying a book in an indecipherable language.
   The first appearance of the wodewose on stage seems to have been at Otford (Kent) in 1348.

WOLF-LIKE CREATURE A large creature, neither dog nor cat, reported in 2004 from Craig y Don, Llandudno, Wales. It was thought to live in nearby woods. [163]

WOLPERTINGER A peculiar animal, variously described, in Bavarian folklore. Sometimes it has wings and fangs. Sometimes it looks like a horned rabbit or squirrel. [182]

WOLUMBIN A kind of apelike creature in the lore of South Australia.

WOLVERHAMPTON WINGED HOMINOID A creature of the mothman kind, seen at Wolverhampton in the evening in March, 2004. Its head was like that of a human, it had two arms to which its wings were attached and two legs. [1]

WOODBURY WATER WITCH Name given to a scaly monster with antennae in this Vermont lake. [N]

WOOKIE Louisiana name for a BHM.

WROCLAW GIANT SNAKE A huge reptile, supposedly killed near Wroclaw, Poland, in 1713. It was said to have exceeded 17' in length. [N E]

WULGARU Human-eating giant of Australian aboriginal belief. [G10]

WURDALAK In Serbian folklore, a werewolf which has died and become a vampire. [156]

WYOMING PTERODACTYL A large-headed creature resembling a pterodactyl seen in a field near Lusk (Wyoming) in 1993.   [157]

XUCURUS CREATURE 9' tall humanoids with antennae or something like them, were reported emerging from a cave at Xucurus in Argentina in 1979. Their legs were said to be square. [187]

YA-TE-VEO TREE Cryptobotanic tree of Central America, which impales its victims and ingests their blood. [179]

YE'I'TSOH The primeval monster of Navaho myth. Some say his father was the sun, some a rock. He is variously known as the Big Monster and the Grey God. Coyote, who features in so many Amerindian myths, is his messenger. [R8]

YELLOW FOX The dead body of such a creature was discovered in Minnesota in 2004. A mustard yellow fox was reportedly seen in Alabama in 1993. [2]

YONG The dragon of Korean mythology. There are three types: the *yong* in the sky, the *yo* in the sea and the *kyo* in the mountains.

YORKSHIRE SEA MONSTER A creature seen off the Yorkshire coast in 1927. It was at first mistaken for a mast and then discovered to be a long neck sticking out of the water. [146]

YURLUNGUR Among the Murrigin Aborigines of Australia, a huge python. [186]

ZEEGANGSA A kind of sea serpent reported from the Java coast, regarded as harmless by the locals. [N]

ZENGKLOBARI Legendary flying creature of New Guinea, perhaps identical with the ropen. [2]

ZERLEG-KHOON A term applied to a hairy hominid in Asia. [179]

ZIGZAG MAN Peculiar monster found in South African cave paintings, perhaps a depiction of some forgotten beast. [173]

ZIPACNA A creature in Mayan mythology with the head of a crocodile. [M11]

ZITNY SMIJ The corn dragon of Lithuanian belief. [171]

ZMEU A creature resembling a dragon with shape shifting ability in Romanian folklore. It was on the dangerous side, for it could spit fire from the sky. [182]

ZOTZILAHA CHAMALCAN A kind of crypto-bat in Mayan lore.

Corrigenda to *Dictionary*

ALBAWITCH Remove *Dictionary* article and replace with the one above.
p.233, line 28, replace "Doglas" with "Dobsenga".

Sources

Source references are to be found in *Dictionary*. New source references are listed below.

Books

A4   Arnold, N. *Alien Zoo* n.p: n.d.

A5   Arment, C. *Cryptozoology: Science and Speculation* Landisville: 2004

B18   Barber, C. *Mysterious Wales* Abergavenny: 2000.

B19   Bernheimer, R. *Wild Men in the Middle Ages* Cambridge (Mass.): 1952

B20   Bartra, R. *Wild Men in the Looking Glass* Ann Arbor: 1994.

D10   Downes, J. *Monster Hunter* Exeter: 2005.

G10   Gilmour, D. *Monsters* Philadelphia: 2003.

G11   Gilroy, R. *Giants from the Dreamtime* Katoomba: 2001.

H15   Hartland, E.S. *County Folklore: Gloucestershire* n.p.: 1895.

H16   Hall, J. *Half Human, Half Animal* Bloomington: 2003.

H17   Hamilton, M. *A New World Bestiary* Vancouver: 1985.

M11   Mott, W.M. *Caverns, cauldrons and Concealed Creatures* Frankston: 2002.

N   Newman, M. *Encyclopaedia of Cryptozoology* Jefferson: 2005.

P3   Pickering, D. *Dictionary of Folklore* London: 1999.

R8   Reichard, G.A. *Navaho Religion* New York: 1950.

S19   Slemen, T. *Tom Slemen's Mysterious World* Liverpool: 2004.

Websites

153 anomalous felids

154 paranormal.about.com

155 www.europacz.com

156 wererat.net

157 CryptoJungle Message Board

158 indianjungle.com

159 www.orkneyjar.com

160 www.dragonorama.com

161 Illinois Cryptozoology Research

162 Mothman 2004

163 www.northwales.icnet.co.uk

164 www.rense.com

165 www.answers.com

166 strange florida

167 www.bigcats.org

168 www.newanimal.org

169 www.ilhawaii.net

170 www.ghostsandcritters.com

171 dragon stone

172 parasearchers.org

173 fort chatroom

174 www.mothmanlives.com

175 www.beesty.ho8.com

176 www.strangestories.co.uk

177 www.bfro.net

178 www.n2.net/prey/bigfoot

179 encyclopedia lurkanika

180 creature team website

181 www.mysticaluniverse.com

182 psych central

183 very hairy dictionary
    (Scott White)

184 www.danu.co.uk

185 www.maria-brazil.org

186 www.geocities.com/
    kondose

187 lost dominion